The creator of Narnia and the most quoted Christian of the 20th Century

C S LEWIS
1898–1963
Author and
Christian apologist

Ronald W Bresland

Day One

Series Editor: Brian H Edwards

Day One

CS Lewis

Meet CS Lewis

Millions of readers identify CS Lewis as the author of the imaginary world of Narnia, the series of seven stories that began in 1950 with *The Lion, the Witch and the Wardrobe* and ended with *The Last Battle* in 1956. *The Chronicles of Narnia* secured his reputation as one of the most popular authors in the history of children's literature. Lewis's works have sold over a hundred million copies and have been translated into more than twenty languages, including Welsh, Chinese, Icelandic, and Hawaiian.

His popularity has continued to grow world-wide. Helped initially by the film *Shadowlands* in 1993 and the more recent film adaptation of *The Lion, the Witch and the Wardrobe* in 2005—the first of Narnian stories to be made into movies. This will ensure that Lewis remains in the public imagination for the foreseeable future.

However, CS Lewis is much more than a successful children's author. He gained a formidable reputation as an Oxford academic, wartime broadcaster, literary critic, poet, science-fiction writer, and man of letters with over thirty books and numerous articles to his credit.

From a self-confessed intellectual atheist, he went on to influence the lives of thousands of Christians and to become one of the greatest Christian writers of the twentieth century. CS Lewis has been described as 'the Aquinas, the Augustine and the Aesop of contemporary evangelicalism' and an 'Apostle to the Skeptics.'

In his book *Mere Christianity* Lewis argued that Jesus was either mad, bad, or indeed exactly who he claimed to be—the Son of the living God!

This book tells the story of CS Lewis' journey from atheism to being one of the most effective communicators of the Christian faith in the world.

Facing page: CS Lewis (on the left) with his brother Warren in 1920

Above: Lewis was infatuated with trains as a child, and when on holiday pestered his mother to take him back to Castlerock station every time he saw a signal down
Below: Castlerock Train Station

Above: Portballintrae on the Causeway Coast which Lewis knew well

A garden in a biscuit tin

The most important spiritual experience of CS Lewis' early life took place in a garden in Belfast. Standing next to a flowering currant bush on a summer day, the young boy suddenly became aware of something he felt he had experienced before—'a memory of a memory'—of a time at Dundela Villas when his brother had presented him with a toy garden made from moss and leaves in an old biscuit tin that triggered feelings of *joy* and longing in him. But longing for what? It was to be many years before he discovered that this spiritual experience was pointing him towards God. The effect on him was startling and he struggled to capture the meaning of the moment: he knew it was a sensation of desire, but he could not grasp what the desire was for. He was certain that it was not for a biscuit-tin filled with moss or even for his past, but before he knew it, the longing vanished and the world was 'turned commonplace again.' The experience had taken only a moment of time and he felt that in a certain sense everything else that had ever happened to him was insignificant in comparison. CS Lewis was however sure of one thing: 'as long as I live, my imagination of Paradise will retain something of my brother's toy garden.'

The effect of this on young Jack Lewis's imagination cannot be overestimated, because it moulded much of his later thought and cleared the way for his eventual acceptance of Christianity. The religious significance of this toy garden reflected for Jack the Biblical Garden of Eden, and the feeling that he was 'returning at last from exile and desert lands to my own country.' It was loaded with Christian symbolism, and

CONTENTS

 First printed 2006

All Scripture quotations are taken from the Authorized Version

A CIP record is held at The British Library ISBN 978 1 84625 056 9

Published by Day One Publications Ryelands Road, Leominster, HR6 8NZ

☎ 01568 613 740 FAX 01568 611 473 email: sales@dayone.co.uk www.dayone.co.uk

Design and Art Direction: Steve Devane Printed by Guttenburg Press, Malta

Dedication: To Catherine—my wife, and Michelle, Gregory, Darryl, Daniel and Emily—my children

Meet CS Lewis

Millions of readers identify CS Lewis as the author of the imaginary world of Narnia, the series of seven stories that began in 1950 with *The Lion, the Witch and the Wardrobe* and ended with *The Last Battle* in 1956. *The Chronicles of Narnia* secured his reputation as one of the most popular authors in the history of children's literature. Lewis's works have sold over a hundred million copies and have been translated into more than twenty languages, including Welsh, Chinese, Icelandic, and Hawaiian.

His popularity has continued to grow world-wide. Helped initially by the film *Shadowlands* in 1993 and the more recent film adaptation of *The Lion, the Witch and the Wardrobe* in 2005—the first of Narnian stories to be made into movies. This will ensure that Lewis remains in the public imagination for the foreseeable future.

However, CS Lewis is much more than a successful children's author. He gained a formidable reputation as an Oxford academic, wartime broadcaster, literary critic, poet, science-fiction writer, and man of letters with over thirty books and numerous articles to his credit.

From a self-confessed intellectual atheist, he went on to influence the lives of thousands of Christians and to become one of the greatest Christian writers of the twentieth century. CS Lewis has been described as 'the Aquinas, the Augustine and the Aesop of contemporary evangelicalism' and an 'Apostle to the Skeptics.'

In his book *Mere Christianity* Lewis argued that Jesus was either mad, bad, or indeed exactly who he claimed to be—the Son of the living God!

This book tells the story of CS Lewis' journey from atheism to being one of the most effective communicators of the Christian faith in the world.

Facing page: *CS Lewis (on the left) with his brother Warren in 1920*

1 Belfast beginnings

From the obscurity of a comfortable middle-class Ulster home to one of the foremost Christian authors of his generation, CS Lewis summed up the early years of his life as containing everything a child needs, 'good parents, good food, and a garden to play in'

'The sound of a steamer's horn at night still conjures up my whole boyhood.' This was how Lewis described the effect of a childhood spent within earshot of the great shipbuilding heart of Belfast. With good reason he was proud of his Ulster birthplace: the Belfast of the early twentieth century was one of the most thriving industrial cities in Western Europe. CS Lewis remarked in later years, somewhat embarrassed by his youthful fervour, of the pleasure he and his brother Warnie gleaned from reminding his English school friends that Belfast boasted not only the largest gantry in the British Isles, but had launched the *Oceanic*—then the largest ship afloat. Lewis would later celebrate Belfast's shipbuilding heritage in the poem 'Of Ships', which captures his childhood experience of returning by boat to Belfast and hearing the familiar hum of the Harland and Wolff shipyard: the sound

'more tunable than song of any bird,
A thousand hammers ringing in the morn.'

It was not only the sounds, but

Above: *Mural in East Belfast by the Lower Newtownards Residents Group celebrating Belfast's most famous writer, CS Lewis*

Facing page: *A Belfast childhood. CS Lewis on the steps of Glenmachan House c.1904*

the sights of Belfast which enchanted the young Lewis brothers: CS Lewis' Belfast was 'a forest of factory chimneys, gantries, and giant cranes rising out of a welter of mist', and his older brother Warren chose 'Sunset over Belfast Lough' for a schoolboy essay assignment as the most beautiful sight he had ever seen. The brothers' most treasured possession was the telescope which stood in their bedroom and which was positioned to take advantage of the view over the shipyards and Belfast Lough.

CS Lewis was also proud of his parentage. On his mother's side, Florence Hamilton's family had a

Above, left: *Richard Lewis, grandfather of CS Lewis, c.1900*
Above, right: *Albert Lewis, father of CS Lewis, c.1902*

Below:*Belfast today with the, now redundant, giant cranes 'Samson' and 'Goliath' of the Harland and Wolff shipyard dominating the skyline*

Above: *Mural in East Belfast depicting Belfast's shipbuilding heritage*

distinguished ancestry that included many generations of clergymen, lawyers, and sailors, and on *her* mother's side, through the Warrens, the blood went back to a Norman knight whose bones lie at Battle Abbey in East Sussex, where the Battle of Hastings was fought in 1066. This same knight is the 'William of Warenne' who appears in Rudyard Kipling's poem *The Land*. The Hamiltons had the quiet confidence in their ancestry that bred a certain self-assuredness, and when the young Clive Staples wrote his first childhood stories, they were partly an imaginative tribute and acknowledgement of the family's proud association with this noble ancestor, and partly an attempt to combine his two main literary pleasures: 'dressed animals' and 'knights-in-armour.'

His father, Albert Lewis, came from more humble stock. The Lewises were farmers from North Wales. His father, Richard Lewis (1832–1908), moved to Ireland in the 1850s and worked as a boilermaker for the Cork Steamship Company before settling in Dublin to take up the position of yard-manager with another shipbuilding firm in 1864. The following year the family moved to Belfast where Richard Lewis entered into a partnership with a colleague from his Dublin workplace to found the firm of MacIlwaine and Lewis, Boiler Makers, Engineers, and Iron Ship

Builders at Abercorn Basin, Belfast.

Significantly, Richard Lewis also composed science-fiction and fantasy stories to amuse his children, one of which features a character called Mr Timothy Tumbledown who advertises for a telescope to 'show the inhabitants of the moon life size.' This combination of his grandfather's interests—Christianity and science fiction—proved to be a strong influence on his grandson, CS Lewis, whose boyhood story 'To Mars and Back' gave a foretaste of the wonderful 'Space Trilogy' which he would write in later life. This fascination with the possibilities that science fiction afforded would lead him to explore God's relationship to his Creation on a truly cosmic scale.

Cautious courting

By the time Albert Lewis began courting Florence Hamilton, the daughter of the minister of his parish, his social expectations were somewhat higher, and his first faltering steps on the road to social advancement were taken with a self-conscious nervousness. Her father, the Rev. Thomas Hamilton, was an outspoken and formidable figure who was well grounded in the evangelical reformed faith—he would often distribute tracts by JC Ryle when copies of the Bible were not

***Above:** Queen's University, Belfast, today. The University plans to pay tribute to CS Lewis by designing a special Reading Room in their new library due to open in 2009*

Above: Detail of a photograph of Flora Lewis (then Florence Hamilton) on her graduation day at Queen's University. She was amongst the first ladies to graduate from Queen's University, Belfast, in 1886, with a first in logic and second class honours in mathematics. Flora is seated in the front row, extreme left

available. From 1870–1874 Thomas Hamilton was Chaplain of Holy Trinity Church in Rome. This was the second Church of England chaplaincy in Rome at the time and was considered 'Low church' in relation to the 'competition' of the rather 'High' All Saints Church. Holy Trinity Church only acquired a building during the period of the First World War and was subsequently destroyed during allied bombing of the city in 1943. Following his time in Rome, Thomas Hamilton returned to Ireland and took up the incumbency of St. Mark's, Dundela, Belfast, a post he held until his retirement in 1900. Thomas Hamilton died on 19 May 1905, aged 79.

The Hamilton family regarded Albert Lewis as perhaps not quite the catch they had hoped for their daughter. However, the young man was obviously in love with Flora and had relatively good social and financial prospects as a solicitor. He had established his own legal practice in Belfast in 1885, and was forging a reputation as a witty and able Conservative politician. The Reverend Thomas Hamilton gave permission for the union and on 29 August 1894, the couple were married by him at St. Mark's Church, Dundela, Belfast.

He is 'Jacksie'

The couple's first child, Warren ('Warnie') Hamilton Lewis was born on 16 June 1895, and on

Thomas Hamilton

Thomas Hamilton graduated from Trinity College, Dublin in 1848 and was ordained the same year. In 1850 he set out on the 'grand tour' of the chief towns and cities of Europe, which was then considered essential in completing a 'gentleman's education.', Arriving in India two years later, he took Priest's orders, probably in Calcutta, in 1853. He served as Chaplain of HMS Royal George with the Baltic squadron of the fleet during the Crimean War. His cabin on board ship measured 9ft by 6ft 4inches and yet he thought he would 'have quite enough room in it.' On examining the crew on their knowledge of the Catechism he concluded, 'I foresee much work here, may I be guided and blessed in it for Jesus' sake.'

Thomas Hamilton records a conversation he had with an Italian priest and university professor, the Rev. Dr Malan, in Geneva in 1851. In the course of their talk, Hamilton asked him the meaning of the name Jesus. Dr Malan smiled at the simplicity of the question and answered, 'A Saviour'.

'What is a Saviour?' queried Hamilton.

'One who saves,' replied Malan, smiling again.

Establishing that it is God who saves and that he does nothing by halves, but completely—or anything that requires being done over again, Hamilton noted that he had him 'under the net.' Hamilton continued, 'If Christ saves completely, then he for whom Christ died can never be lost.' Malan was somewhat taken aback by this, but after some hesitation agreed.

'Now you are no longer a Romanist' announced Hamilton to the silent priest who was now deep in thought. To the question of what he now thought of the Mass, Malan had to agree that since what Christ had done could not be repeated, then purgatory, indulgences, and such like must necessarily be wrong. The conversation ended with Thomas Hamilton's observation: 'He left the Church of Rome.'

Pictured: *The Rev. Thomas Hamilton, CS Lewis's maternal grandfather, portrait in oils by the artist AR Baker*

29 November 1898, Clive Staples Lewis followed. At the age of four CS Lewis decided that his name was 'Jacksie,' later shortened to 'Jack,' and he refused to answer to any other. That was the name by which he was known for the rest of his life.

Jack was born into a family that enjoyed relative financial security, a comfortable home, annual seaside holidays, servants—including a gardener, nursemaid, governess, cook, and a housemaid. The Lewis family first lived in the more densely populated and working class area of East Belfast in the semi-

***Above:** The Lewis family in 1899. From left to right, front row: CS Lewis' uncle Augustus ('Gussie') Hamilton with baby, Martha Gee Lewis (grandmother), Albert James Lewis (father) with his sons, Warren and baby Clive Staples on lap, Anne ('Annie') Harley Hamilton (aunt). Back Row: Richard Lewis (grandfather), Eileen Lewis (cousin), Flora Lewis (mother), Leonard Lewis (cousin) and Agnes Young Lewis (aunt)*

detached Dundela Villas, until they moved in 1905 to the new house, 'Little Lea', in the affluent Circular Road, not far from Dundela.

One of the highlights of Jack and Warnie's childhood was the annual seaside holiday with their mother, normally to the seaside resort of Castlerock, County Londonderry, where they would stay for up to six weeks at a time. They also visited the nearby resorts of Downhill, Portrush and Ballycastle. We know from the later accounts of Jack and Warren that their parents were extremely cautious regarding the boys' health and would have considered a seaside holiday beneficial.

Albert confined his visits during these periods to the occasional weekend. Warren Lewis has described the excitement he and Jack felt when the great moment of the horse drawn cab arrived to take the family to the railway station, and one of his abiding memories of these holidays was the contrast between the family's excitement and preparation for the holiday and his father's gloomy detachment.

The earliest indication of CS Lewis' love of swimming in the sea can be found in a letter from 1901 in which his mother informed her husband Albert (affectionately addressed as 'Dear Bear' or 'Old Bear') that, 'Baby was very anxious to get into the water.' It was these childhood holidays of sand and sea that instilled in Lewis a love of surf-bathing that remained with him throughout his life. This was apparently shared by his grandfather, Thomas Hamilton, who was causing concern and alarm within the family by insisting, regardless of the cold, on swimming at Castlerock, even though he was aged 74 at the time!

These childhood holidays introduced Lewis to a sense of the geography of Ulster and the wider landscape which he was to incorporate into his early stories and drawings that so absorbed his imagination. Indeed, the attachment CS Lewis felt for this area can be seen in the impression it had on his imagination: the whole concept of 'Northernness' that was so important to him, and to which he refers in *Surprised by Joy*, owes a great deal to the imaginative influence of the rugged coastline of the Causeway and Donegal coasts.

From the vantage point of the Ulster coastline, Lewis experienced the sensation of 'Northernness' and compared it to 'a vision of huge clear spaces

Left: *The site where Albert Lewis' legal offices once stood in Royal Avenue, Belfast*

Above: *It is significant that the caricature of Albert Lewis that appears in Ireland's Saturday Night newspaper in 1921 shows him holding an academic 'mortar board' under one arm and a volume entitled 'English Literature' under the other, the significance being that he was apparently as well known as a literary man as he was a solicitor*

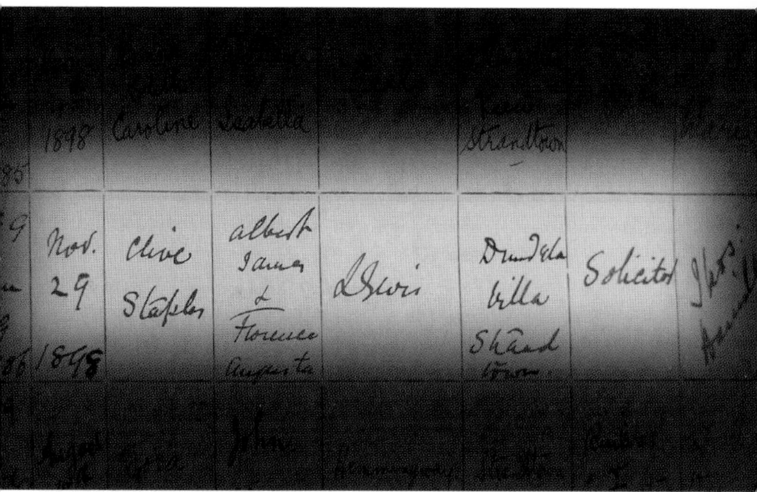

1898 Caroline Isabella Strandtown

Nov. 29 1898 Clive Staples Albert James & Florence Augusta Lewis Dundela Villa Strand Town Solicitor

Above: *Baptismal entry for CS Lewis*

Left: *St Mark's Church of Ireland, Dundela, where Albert and Florence Lewis were married in 1894 by her father, the Reverend Thomas Hamilton, and where 'Jack' and his brother were baptised*

hanging above the Atlantic in the endless twilight of Northern summer.' He describes how, from an early age, this sense of 'Northernness' stirred within him indescribable feelings of sadness and longing for vast empty spaces and cold remote places. He had read of places such as these in the stories of William Morris and the tales from Norse mythology. He was also deeply moved by the music of Richard Wagner, whose operas dramatised episodes from the Norse sagas and which he felt captured the essence of his feelings for 'Northernness' in a way in which words could not.

The birth of an imagination

The Lewis family's decision to move in 1905 to the Circular Road area of Belfast was partly motivated (like their earlier choice of holiday destination) by concern for the health of their two sons. A report into the state of public health in Belfast was conducted in 1906 and found that the annual death rate from tuberculosis was more than double that of England and Wales and much worse than that of Dublin. In addition, poor sanitary conditions resulted in Belfast having the highest death rate from typhoid in the whole of Britain.

To the young CS Lewis, Little Lea 'seemed less like a house than a city' and it was here that his first stories were written and illustrated with 'enormous satisfaction'. The view from their front door was very different from what it is today: in 1905 they 'looked down over wide fields to Belfast Lough and across it to the long mountain line of the Antrim shore—Divis, Colin, and the Cave Hill.' The beauty of the 'summer sunsets behind these blue ridges, and the rooks flying home', made a lasting impression on Lewis and marked the beginnings of his love affair with Belfast. The wetness of Irish weather and the nervousness of Jack's and Warren's parents about damp and exposure to the elements meant that, as Warren records, '[We] spent an extraordinary amount of time shut up indoors.' He describes how they would gaze out of the nursery window at the slanting

Left: *The baptismal font at the west end of St Mark's Church, Dundela, Belfast. CS Lewis was baptised here by his grandfather, the Rev. Thomas Hamilton, on 29 January 1899*

Above: *Mussenden Temple, at Downhill, not far from Castlerock, dominates the landscape. The building was originally intended as a library and was built by Frederick Hervey (1768–1803), Bishop of Derry. CS Lewis and his brother Warren walked to Downhill from Castlerock when on holiday with their mother, and returned to the area in later life*

rain and grey skies, past a sodden meadow, to the strange and distant land beyond.

It was during these wet afternoons that Jack Lewis began to develop his imagination and discover the world of literature. From his childhood he was an enthusiastic reader. In later life he recalled that at the age of six, seven and eight he was reading Beatrix Potter's books, E Nesbit's fantasy trilogy, Swift's *Gulliver's Travels* and much more; by the age of nine, young Jack recorded in his diary his first encounter with John Milton's epic poem on the Fall of Man: 'I read *Paradise Lost*, reflections thereon.' Of his boyhood Lewis confessed, 'I was living almost entirely in my imagination.'

Jack was schooled at home in French and Latin by his mother, and 'everything else' by his governess, a Presbyterian lady called Annie Harper. One day, between sums and writing, she gave an impromptu lecture on spiritual things: Lewis later wrote that the talk was the first thing he could remember that 'brought the other world' to his mind 'with any sense of reality.'

Above: *Lewis was infatuated with trains as a child, and when on holiday pestered his mother to take him back to Castlerock station every time he saw a signal down*

Left: *Castlerock Train Station*

Above: Portballintrae on the Causeway Coast which Lewis knew well

A garden in a biscuit tin

The most important spiritual experience of CS Lewis' early life took place in a garden in Belfast. Standing next to a flowering currant bush on a summer day, the young boy suddenly became aware of something he felt he had experienced before—'a memory of a memory'—of a time at Dundela Villas when his brother had presented him with a toy garden made from moss and leaves in an old biscuit tin that triggered feelings of *joy* and longing in him. But longing for what? It was to be many years before he discovered that this spiritual experience was pointing him towards God. The effect on him was startling and he struggled to capture the meaning of the moment: he knew it was a sensation of desire, but he could not grasp what the desire was for. He was certain that it was not for a biscuit-tin filled with moss or even for his past, but before he knew it, the longing vanished and the world was 'turned commonplace again.' The experience had taken only a moment of time and he felt that in a certain sense everything else that had ever happened to him was insignificant in comparison. CS Lewis was however sure of one thing: 'as long as I live, my imagination of Paradise will retain something of my brother's toy garden.'

The effect of this on young Jack Lewis's imagination cannot be overestimated, because it moulded much of his later thought and cleared the way for his eventual acceptance of Christianity. The religious significance of this toy garden reflected for Jack the Biblical Garden of Eden, and the feeling that he was 'returning at last from exile and desert lands to my own country.' It was loaded with Christian symbolism, and suggested that even at this young age he had absorbed something valuable from the Christianity of his childhood. When Lewis embraced Christianity in later life he would recognise these early events as being significant spiritual signposts, though they were not the thing itself. As he later referred to it: 'not the wave but the wave's imprint on the sand.'

However, these spiritual pointers were not fully understood as such, and it was to be many

The beginnings of a literary career

CS Lewis confessed that what drove him to write was the 'extreme manual clumsiness' he suffered from having only one joint in the thumb—a defect he inherited from his father and shared with his brother—which left him with 'an utter incapacity to make anything.' He longed to make things, but after many tears and failed attempts with cardboard and scissors, he found something he could do—hold a pen! His love of stories led him to write his own. Young Jack Lewis soon found that he had been admitted to 'a world of happiness' and found that 'you can do more with a castle in a story than with the best cardboard castle that ever stood on a nursery table.'

If Belfast at the beginning of the twentieth century could lay claim to being 'the most literate corner of Ireland' then the Lewis household was an extravagant testimony to the truth of this. Jack describes Little Lea as overflowing with books reflecting his parents' varied interests, and that he had 'the same certainty of finding a book that was new to me as a man who walks into a field has of finding a new blade of grass.' The young Lewis brothers could not help but be influenced by such an environment: Jack's stories of 'Animal-Land' combined with his brother Warren's stories on 'India' (probably inspired by his grandfather Hamilton's accounts of his time as a minister in Calcutta), and they culminated in the remarkable world they named Boxen.

The brothers found an eager audience for this work in the family literary magazine called 'The Leeborough Review' which was compiled, with the encouragement and help of their parents, for their own amusement. The stories were given an added dimension by the use of maps and drawings to enliven this elaborately invented world populated by, amongst others, an aristocratic frog, a rabbit king, and an artistic owl. In mapping and chronicling these imaginary worlds, CS Lewis was training himself to be a writer.

Pictured: *Painting of CS Lewis' first childhood home, Dundela Villas, painted from memory by the Belfast artist, Alan Seaton. It was here, as a child, that Lewis began his adventure into literature*

Above: *The Giant's Causeway on the North Antrim coast is, like Mount Everest and the Giant Redwoods of California, a World Heritage site*

Below: *Christ Church, Church of Ireland, Castlerock. The Lewis family would have attended here whilst on holiday*

years before he appreciated their importance. This childhood experience of joy changed his life for ever. CS Lewis probably had this event in mind when, over thirty years later, he spoke of childhood and how children can remember events, well before adults thought them capable of 'understanding' anything; in his own case, he already had 'spiritual experiences as pure and as momentous as any … undergone since.'

Above: The Castlerock beach holiday was the highlight of the year for the Lewis children *Below:* The stained glass window of St Columb and St. Patrick in Church of Ireland Church, Castlerock. CS Lewis once wrote 'I was born in Holy Ireland, where there are no snakes because St Patrick sent them all away.'

TRAVEL INFORMATION

St Mark's Church, (Church of Ireland)

and The Old Rectory, Dundela, Holywood Road, Belfast

www.dundela.down.anglican.org ☎ 028 9065 4090

CS Lewis' local church in which he was baptised on 29 January 1899 and confirmed on 6 December 1914. There is a stained glass window in the church, donated by the Lewis brothers in memory of their parents, designed by the Irish artist Michael Healy. The Old Rectory is beside St Mark's Church and was the home of Lewis' grandfather, the Reverend Thomas Hamilton, until his death in 1905.

The Searcher, Holywood Road Library

Holywood Arches, 4–12 Holywood Road, Belfast http://www.ni-libraries.net

☎ 028 90 509216

The CS Lewis centenary sculpture by Northern Irish artist Ross Wilson is an inspired creation which is based on the literary character of Digory Kirke, who, in the Narnia story, *The Magician's Nephew*, has the wardrobe made from a beautiful apple tree which has special properties. It is through

KEY TO PLACES

1 ST MARK'S CHURCH

2 LITTLE LEA

3 SITE OF 'BERNAGH' (NOW DEMOLISHED)

4 DUNDELA FLATS

5 HOLYWOOD ROAD LIBRARY AND SCULPTURE

6 CAMPBELL COLLEGE

7 BELMONT TOWER

Above: *Little Lea, the Lewis family home from 1905 until 1930, when it was sold following the death of Albert Lewis. There is a poignant account of the Lewis brothers' last visit there and packing their childhood toys in a box which they then buried in the garden*

this magical wardrobe that the Pevensie children, Peter, Susan, Edmund and Lucy, enter Narnia and meet the talking animals and mythological creatures that populate that snowbound world. Modelled on CS Lewis as he was in 1919, the sculpture seeks, in the words of the artist, to capture the 'great ideas of sacrifice, redemption, victory, and freedom for the Sons of Adam and the Daughters of Eve' that lie at the heart of the Chronicles of Narnia.

Dundela Flats, Dundela Avenue, Belfast

Dundela Flats now occupy the site of what was once Albert and Flora Lewis's Belfast home 'Dundela Villas'. The pair of semi-detached houses was attached to an old coach house. The couple moved here following their marriage in 1894 and saw both their sons born here. The houses were demolished in 1952.

The Queen's University of Belfast

University Road, Belfast

http://www.qub.ac.uk
☎ 02890 245133
CS Lewis' mother, Flora Lewis, was a brilliant student who attended The Queen's University of Belfast (then The Royal University of Ireland) where she studied Geometry, Algebra, Logic and Mathematics before receiving her BA in 1886.

Left: The Queen's University of Belfast

Bottom: The Searcher centenary sculpture which stands outside the Holywood Arches Library, East Belfast, not far from Little Lea

Below: The CS Lewis Centenary Group Blue Plaque at Dundela flats marks the birthplace of CS Lewis

C S Lewis Centenary Group
C S LEWIS
1898–1963
Author and
Christian apologist
born
on this site

Whilst studying at Queen's she also attended 'Ladies' Classes' in the nearby Methodist College from 1881 to 1885. CS Lewis discussed with his brother the possibility of finding employment here and mused on the possibility of keeping their home in Oxford as a holiday destination.

Linen Hall Library
17 Donegall Square North, Belfast

http://www.linenhall.com
☎ 028 9032 1707
The Linen Hall Library is home to a unique collection of books by and about CS Lewis. The collection, donated by the CS Lewis Association of Ireland, is a first for Northern Ireland and is a fitting tribute to one of Belfast's most famous literary figures. Originally founded in 1788 as The Belfast Reading Society, in 1801 it was established as the Belfast Library and Society for Promoting Knowledge. Not only is it Belfast's oldest library, but it is also the last subscription library in Ireland.

2 Fatal breaks

The death of his mother, the beginnings of a rift with his father, and the upheaval of leaving his home and country, all contributed to CS Lewis' acute unhappiness. He was tutored by 'The Great Knock'—and abandoned the Christian faith

One August night in 1908, when young Jack Lewis was crying with the pain of headache and toothache, he called from his bed for his mother—but his mother was much too ill to come. The nine year old was vaguely aware of noises within the house: the sounds of whispered voices, hurried footsteps, doors opening and closing, and of doctors and nurses coming and going. He became increasingly distressed. Then—the moment he would remember for the rest of his adult life—his father, in tears, entering the room and attempting to convey to the terrified boy the awful news that his mother was dead.

The tranquil existence which Jack and Warnie had enjoyed at Little Lea was shattered by the death of Florence Lewis after a long and painful battle with abdominal cancer. For Albert Lewis, his wife's death was a devastating blow, and one from which he never fully recovered. Apart from the death of his wife on the day of his forty-fifth birthday, Albert also lost his elder brother Joseph two weeks later, and his father earlier in the same year. Albert marked the event by

Above: *Flora Lewis, who died when Jack was just nine years old. Her death changed his world forever*

Facing page: *Lighthouse at St John's Point in Lecale, County Down. Flora Lewis took Jack and Warnie here as children in 1905 and they were thrilled when the men 'lit up' for them and showed them around the lighthouse*

preserving the leaf from the Shakespearean calendar which hung in Flora's room. It read for that day: 'Men must endure their going hence, even as their coming hither: Ripeness is all.'

The loss of his wife left Albert Lewis, in his own words, 'broken and inert' and ill-equipped to comfort his grieving sons. The aftermath of this bereavement marked the beginning of a rift in relations between the three. The death of his mother was a terrifying episode in young Jack's life, and in his autobiography, *Surprised by Joy*, he describes not only the fear of losing his mother, but the crucial change in attitude towards his father. The whole traumatic experience had the effect of drawing Jack and Warnie closer together as brothers, whilst at the same time alienating them from their father. Jack saw himself as being very much on his own from this point and summed it up like this: 'With my mother's death, all settled happiness–all that was tranquil and reliable–disappeared from my life.'

Two 'abominable places'

This was only the beginning of the difficulties which would now face the young CS Lewis. Within two weeks of his mother's death, Jack returned with his brother to England to attend Wynyard House boarding school in Watford, where Warnie was already a pupil. Any greater wrench is hard to imagine. A young grieving boy sent off, within a fortnight of his mother's death, to a strange country and an even stranger school. Albert was struggling to come to terms with the death of his wife, and was suffering great emotional strain when he decided it would be best to proceed with the plans to send Jack back to

Above: *The grave of Flora and Albert Lewis in Belfast City Cemetery*

***Above:** Jack and Warnie sailed out of Belfast Lough and crossed the Irish Sea up to six times each year as schoolboys*

England with Warnie. These plans had been previously discussed and agreed between Albert, Flora and the man who was to have the greatest impact on Jack's education, WT Kirkpatrick. This trusted friend had been Albert's former headmaster at Lurgan College in County Armagh and his views helped decide the matter of Jack's future.

This decision to send the Lewis brothers to a public school in England was motivated by a number of reasons. Naturally they wanted their boys to receive the best possible education, but whilst this was a high priority, class and the desire that their sons should advance on the social ladder were considered equally important. Flora Lewis had previously expressed concern that her sons should adopt the best 'accent' and the attendant social graces that such an education offered. Albert Lewis also hoped that by sending Jack to a public school he would break down his shyness and his 'morbid desire for isolation and seclusion'; these he acknowledged had been part of his own inadequacies and threatened to be even stronger in Jack.

When Jack joined his brother Warnie at Wynyard House School in Watford, his initial reaction to England was one of horror. The train journey from Fleetwood to Euston revealed: 'The miles and miles of featureless land, shutting one in from the sea, imprisoning, suffocating!'

The new school was situated in 'Green Hertfordshire' but, it was not green to a boy bred in County Down, and he later wrote, 'I found myself in a world to which I reacted with immediate hatred.' His distaste was not lessened by the eighteen months he spent at the school. Jack's experience at Wynyard is well documented in his autobiography and a general impression of his time there is revealed by the title of the chapter relating to it, 'Concentration Camp' and the pseudonym used for the school in the book—'Belsen'!

By the time Lewis joined the school in September 1908, the headmaster of Wynyard, the Rev. Robert Capron, 'Oldie' as he was known among his pupils, had already been examined by a brain specialist who found him to be 'mad.' Warnie recalls witnessing Capron hold a boy of twelve at arms length and by the back of his collar with one hand—'as one might a dog'—while using the other free hand to vigorously cane the unfortunate youth around the

The Welsh Connection

CS Lewis described his father's people as 'true Welshmen, sentimental, passionate, and rhetorical …' Jack inherited some measure of the rhetorical ability, for which the Lewis family were noted, from his Welsh ancestors. The earliest known reference to the Welsh heritage is to Edward and Mary Lewis of Rhanberfedd (near the village of Hope in Denbighshire) and their son Thomas, who was born at nearby Gresford in 1747. Thomas married Elizabeth Jones in Hope Parish Church in 1768 and the couple had eight children. It was their son Richard Lewis (1769–1845) who was CS Lewis' great-great-grandfather. Richard Lewis was a Welsh farmer from the North Wales village of Caergwrle, then a small town of 1700 inhabitants, in Flintshire.

He had seven children, one of whom, Joseph Lewis (1802–1890), was an outspoken and impressive preacher. Joseph Lewis moved across the English border to a smallholding at Saltney, now a suburb of Chester, and subsequently to Sandycroft, Flint. He seceded from the Church of England due to his not being given the prominence which he thought his due, and became a minister with the local Primitive Methodist church. His reputation can be gauged by the fact that, nearly thirty years after his death, he was still remembered and referred to locally as 'the grand old man of Methodism.'

His son Richard (1832–1908), moved to Ireland in the 1850's and lived in Cork and Dublin, before the family moved to Belfast. Richard Lewis' Primitive Methodist upbringing had nurtured a concern for the educational, social and spiritual well being of his fellow workers and he was responsible for establishing one of the first working-men's co-operative societies in Cork in the 1860's. Richard Lewis also wrote essays of a theological nature with titles such as 'Essay on a Special Providence' and 'Jonah's Mission to Nineveh' and he read these to fellow workers in the Cork Steamship Company.

Pictured: *Richard Lewis spent the last years of his life at Little Lea until his death in 1908*

Above: *Church of Saint John the Evangelist, Watford, where Lewis regularly attended during his time at Wynyard House School. The church, Lewis observed, 'wanted to be Roman Catholic, but was afraid to say so'*

thighs. The Lewis brothers heartily detested the place, but Jack's letters to his father to remove them from 'this hole' fell on deaf ears. It was not until the school was closed in 1910, due to falling numbers, that Jack finally managed to escape. Capron was eventually put under restraint, certified insane and died in Camberwell House Asylum, Peckham, Kent the following year. He is buried in Watford Cemetery.

Yet, it was not all unremitting horror. The most important thing that happened to Jack at this school was that he became an 'effective believer' in the doctrines of Christianity as distinct from, what Warnie had once called, 'the dry husks of religion offered by the semi-political church-going of Ulster.' Jack credits this early 'conversion' to the church he was obliged to attend—twice every Sunday—whilst at Wynyard. Saint John's in Watford was part of the Church of England and high 'Anglo-Catholic': Jack's initial reaction was to describe the place as 'an abominable place of Romish hypocrites, where people cross themselves [and] bow to what they have the vanity to call an altar.' Whilst Lewis's initial response would have been in line with the sentiments of Grandfather Hamilton, it was not held with any real conviction. Among the positive experiences he took from his time at St. John's was a renewed interest in reading his Bible and a conscious effort to pray seriously.

A welcome relief

Following the death of their mother, the boys found some consolation in the love they were shown by the Ewart family. When one considers that Florence Lewis was related to one of the most influential families in Belfast, it is easier to understand Albert Lewis' cautious courting. Florence Hamilton's cousin and closest friend was Lady Ewart, wife of Sir William Quartus Ewart, a wealthy Belfast linen manufacturer and one of the city's most prominent industrialists. It was at their lavish mansion, Glenmachan, less than a mile from Little Lea, that the Lewis boys had a standing invitation to visit when home from school in England, and it was to this hospitality that Jack credited whatever courtesy and social graces he and Warnie possessed.

The Ewart daughters, Hope, Gundreda and Kelsie, took the motherless boys to their heart and made a significant impact on them. They would play in the glen close to the house and enjoy rides in a donkey-trap. Jack and Warren greatly appreciated the kindness of all the daughters, but reserved their utmost praise for Gundreda, who could not only make them laugh by her skill in mimicking the County Down accent, but was, they agreed, 'the most beautiful woman' they had ever seen. Though Glenmachan was comparable to life at Little Lea in many ways, assured wealth afforded a lifestyle that eluded the Lewis family. Jack's subtle distinction sums up the gulf: 'Life there was more spacious and considered than with us, it glided like a barge where ours bumped like a cart.'

New schools and the loss of faith

Whilst Warnie was able to leave Wynyard school in July 1909, Jack had to remain at Wynyard until its closure in 1910. At this point

Above: *CS Lewis and Kelso ('Kelsie') Ewart on the steps of Glenmachan in 1906. Kelsie (1886–1966) was the second cousin of Jack's mother, Flora Lewis*

Left: *Glenmachan (c.1903) The family home of Sir William Quartus Ewart. CS Lewis refers to the house as 'Mountbracken' and credits Lady Ewart, his mother's cousin and dearest friend, for 'civilising' him and his brother Warren*

Albert, now that the school was permanently closed, responded to his son's systematic pleas for release, and brought Jack home to begin the autumn term at Campbell College, Belfast. The school was about a mile from Little Lea and was named after Henry James Campbell, who left a large estate for the founding of a school 'for the purpose of giving therein a superior liberal Protestant education.' Jack was delighted with his father's decision, and as a boarder he enjoyed the added bonus of being allowed home every Sunday. The most important intellectual event for Jack was his introduction to Matthew Arnold's narrative poem, *Sohrab and Rustum*, by Lewis Alden, the Senior English Master. Alden was known affectionately by his pupils as 'Octie' because his eyes would swell up like those of an octopus when roused to anger.

Lewis' account of being abducted by a gang of boys and hurled down a chute only to emerge into a dark, cramped coal cellar is, along with fonder

Top: *Campbell College c. 1910. The college had been founded, according to Lewis, 'for the express purpose of giving boys all the advantages of a public school education without the trouble of crossing the Irish Sea.' Lewis attended here for part of a term in 1910*

Above: *Cherbourg House, subsequently renamed Ellerslie, the preparatory school in Malvern where Jack lost his Christian faith*

memories of the English master, among the chief impressions of his time there. Out-of-school hours were spent trying to negotiate the milling throng of pupils, and Lewis likened the experience to 'living permanently in a large railway station.' However, halfway through his first term, he fell ill and was removed from the school, thus ending his brief spell within the Irish school system. Following a blissful six-week convalescence at home, occupied with reading, drawing, and the Christmas holidays, Jack returned to England with Warnie to begin a new school.

In January 1911 both boys set off to their respective schools. Warnie was already attending Malvern College, Worcestershire, and it was decided that Jack should go to the nearby preparatory school, Cherbourg House. It was here that Jack lost whatever grasp of the Christian faith he had.

The school Matron, Miss Cowie was loved by all the boys for her cheerful and companionable nature, especially by the 'orphan' Jack. However, her attempts at finding spiritual truth had unwittingly introduced ideas of spirits 'other than God and men' into Jack's mind which would temporarily destroy his faith. She was, he later realised, 'floundering in the mazes of Theosophy, Rosicrucianism, Spiritualism and the whole Anglo-American Occultist tradition.' Miss Cowie, as Jack put it, 'could not tell that the room which she brought the candle into was full of gunpowder' and innocently and unintentionally introduced a speculative character to conversations regarding faith that gradually unravelled Jack's hitherto sincere belief in Christianity. However, despite the spiritual turmoil of this time, he won a classical entrance scholarship to Malvern College, and joined his brother there in 1913.

Jack did not share Warnie's enthusiastic account of life at Malvern, and found it unbearable. His passion was music and

Above: Malvern College, Worcestershire, c. 1914

Above: Amidst the misery he felt at Malvern, Lewis wrote to his new friend, Arthur Greeves, 'County Down must be looking glorious just now: I can just picture the view of the Lough and Cave Hill from beside the Shepherd's Hut.' The view of Belfast as seen from the Holywood Hills to which Lewis is referring

literature and he had little interest in the compulsory games that were actively encouraged in the college. The 'fagging' system that was common in many English public schools–where the younger boys would act as servants to the older boys–meant he was frequently picked on and spent his time there exhausted 'both in body and mind'.

Two events occurred in the Easter holidays of 1914 that were to have a significant and far-reaching impact on Jack Lewis's life. First, his father, finally realising that Jack's letters from Malvern College begging to be removed were motivated by a genuine unhappiness that refused to abate whilst he remained there, made the sensible decision not to return Jack to Malvern for the following year. Instead he was to go to Albert's old headmaster from Lurgan College, WT Kirkpatrick, who now worked as a private tutor in Surrey and had successfully 'crammed' Warnie for the Military Academy at Sandhurst the previous year. The only condition attached to this arrangement was that Jack would have to endure the final summer term at Malvern before joining Kirkpatrick in September of that year.

The second significant event was that during the Easter break Jack decided to take up an

Arthur Greeves (1895–1966)

Arthur Greeves was the youngest of five children. His father, Joseph Malcolmson Greeves, was a member of the Plymouth Brethren and director of the firm J and TM Greeves Ltd, Flax Spinners, Belfast. The family lived at 'Bernagh' just across the road from Little Lea and were the Lewis' nearest neighbours.

CS Lewis' lifelong friendship with Arthur Greeves was instrumental in clarifying ideas about himself and his work. The letters from Jack to his friend provided a platform for debate and literary exploration.

Arthur was not merely a foil for Jack's intellectual superiority: he too had a poetic sensibility and an artistic attentiveness to the natural world that rejoiced in, what he termed, the 'homely'. Arthur would gently direct Jack's attention from intellectual speculations on the nature of the infinite to the natural 'ordinary' beauty of their surroundings. Arthur shared with Jack his love for the countryside of County Down, whilst taking great delight in pointing out everyday scenes; whether they were an old woman returning, bucket in hand, from the pigsty, or a bright hearth seen through an open door as they passed on their walk, or the beauty of a deserted farmyard in early morning solitude.

The Lewis brothers offer differing impressions of Arthur's character: Warnie gives a caustic account of Arthur Greeves, criticizing his lack of self-control, lack of self-reliance, and generally pampered upbringing; Jack gives a more sympathetic account, observing that whilst he himself failed miserably in teaching Arthur to be arrogant, Arthur succeeded in teaching him charity.

Pictured: *Arthur Greeves. The two first met in April 1914 and remained close friends throughout their lives The letters from CS Lewis to Arthur Greeves comprise the largest collection of letters he ever wrote to anyone and provided an unchanging link with his Ulster homeland*

invitation to visit the son of his father's friend and nearest neighbour, Joseph Greeves, who was convalescing from an illness. The boy's name was Arthur Greeves, and on discovering that they both were avid admirers of *Myths of the Norsemen* by HMA Guerber, they struck up an immediate friendship that was to last throughout their lifetime. Their first meeting left an indelible impression on Jack, who expressed his astonishment that there do exist people 'very, very like himself.'

Great Bookham, Surrey

On 19 September 1914 Jack arrived at Great Bookham, Surrey, to take up residence as a boarder with his future tutor. It was with a

***Above:** Fort Royal Hotel, Rathmullan, was a frequent destination for CS Lewis and Arthur Greeves during the 1950s*

certain nervousness that the young man, now approaching his sixteenth year, prepared to meet the almost mythical figure of WT Kirkpatrick, known as 'The Great Knock', eulogised so incessantly by his father, and whose sentiments were now being echoed by his brother.

Jack offers a vivid picture of his first meeting with his new tutor: expecting to find the sentimental and affectionate individual of his father's fond reminiscences. He was startled by Kirkpatrick's abrupt interrogation of his most casual remark on the Surrey countryside. In the course of Jack's increasingly faltering attempts to engage him in general conversation, it soon dawned on him that Kirkpatrick held the idea that for humans to exercise their vocal organs for any purpose other than that of communicating or discovering truth was preposterous. He was, as Jack noted, as near to being a 'purely logical entity' as was humanly possible. Kirkpatrick was over six feet tall, lean and muscular, dressed like a gardener in shabby clothes, and he sported a moustache and side whiskers with a clean-shaven chin 'like the Emperor Franz Joseph.'

The routine adopted at Bookham suited Jack admirably and he declared to his friend Arthur Greeves that he was going to have the time of his life. A normal day would begin with an early rise at seven-thirty, breakfast at eight (usually variations of an Ulster fry with 'good Irish soda-bread on the table'), a quick walk in the garden, and then down to work till one o'clock with a short break, for a cup of tea at eleven. After lunch a good walk till four when he would be back for afternoon tea then back to his desk and work until seven when dinner was served. Then talk, letter writing, and reading until bedtime. Jack said of this typical

Above: The only known photograph of WT Kirkpatrick and his wife Louisa at their home in Great Bookham, Surrey, in October 1920. The house no longer exists

Bookham routine, that if he could please himself, he would always live as he lived during this period.

Lewis thrived under this regime and devoured the Greek and Latin texts which Kirkpatrick would chant in his 'purest Ulster' brogue. His method was to read aloud the first twenty or so lines of a text, then translate it into English, hand Jack a lexicon and leave him to get on with it. Any other pupil would have found this muscular approach daunting, but not Jack who regarded it as 'red beef and strong beer.' His time with Kirkpatrick was one of the happiest of his life and it was the 'Great Knock' that Lewis credited with supplying him with 'mental muscle.' The depth of gratitude that he owed him is acknowledged in Lewis' autobiography, where he

William Thompson Kirkpatrick 'The Great Knock' (1848–1921)

WT Kirkpatrick was born in the townland of Carrickmaddyroe, Boardmills, County Down in 1848. He was educated at the Royal Belfast Academical Institution and Queen's College (now Queen's University), Belfast. He graduated from here in 1868 with a first class honours degree in English, History, and Metaphysics and an MA in 1870. He returned to his old school, Royal Belfast Academical Institution, to take up his first teaching post as Assistant Master in the English Department in 1868 following his first degree. In the same year he entered the Assembly's College, the Presbyterian seminary, in Belfast.

Kirkpatrick completed the necessary three years in theological studies required for ordination into the Irish Presbyterian Church and was granted his licentiate but was never ordained. When Jack knew him he had already declared himself an atheist. However, one curious trait from his Presbyterian upbringing survived: his new pupil wryly noted that whilst Kirkpatrick spent most of his time in the garden, he always, on Sundays, gardened in a different, and slightly more respectable suit, adding, 'An Ulster Scot may come to disbelieve in God, but not to wear his week-day clothes on the Sabbath.' CS Lewis based the character of MacPhee in his novel *That Hideous Strength* on his old tutor.

Above: *St Nicolas Church, Great Bookham. The earliest parts of the church date back to the 11th century and the church is mentioned in the Domesday Book. The novelist Jane Austen visited the church often when her godfather was vicar there*

devoted an entire chapter to Kirkpatrick.

Losing faith

Whilst Kirkpatrick never attacked religion in Jack's presence, he was a 'Rationalist' of what Lewis calls 'the old, high and dry nineteenth century type.' Kirkpatrick's atheism went a considerable way to reinforce his young charge's growing dissatisfaction with his own Christian faith, and whilst he opened up Jack's mind to the richness of classical and other literatures, his own loss of faith and logical mind helped form Lewis' atheistic outlook. The fact that Jack attended St Nicolas Church in Great Bookham every Sunday, despite later claims that his own 'Atheism and Pessimism were fully formed' before he went to Bookham, suggests something of the spiritual muddle he was in.

It was against this background that CS Lewis committed, what he later called, 'one of the worst acts of my life' in allowing himself to be prepared for confirmation, confirmed, and attending his first Communion in St Mark's church, Dundela, Belfast, on 6 December 1914, in total disbelief and merely to please his father and avoid argument.

When Lewis eventually became a Christian, he described how his cowardice in approaching his father on the subject had driven him to hypocrisy, and from hypocrisy to blasphemy. He always felt a sense of guilt over this, and in later years he went some way to make amends for it by advising his God-daughter not to expect or demand all the feelings she would like to have in her first Communion, adding, 'You may, of course: but also you may not. But don't worry if you don't get them. They aren't what matter.'

Left: *Interior of St Mark's Church, Dundela, Belfast. Sir John Betjeman, a leading authority on architecture, particularly Victorian Church architecture (and a former pupil of CS Lewis' at Magdalen College) described St Mark's as 'Butterfield at his best.'*

TRAVEL INFORMATION

The Parish Church of St Nicolas, Bookham

Lower Road, Great Bookham, Surrey KT23 4AT
myweb.tiscali.co.uk/St.Nicholas.Church

St Nicolas was one of the most universally venerated saints in Christendom and attempts have been made to make him one of the church leaders at the Council of Nicea (AD 325). There are many stained-glass windows, frescoes, and carvings, depicting the cycle of his life in Europe and in various English churches, including the font at Winchester cathedral and on an ivory crosier head at the Victoria and Albert Museum. His cult would eventually give rise to the institution of what we now know as 'Santa Claus.' There are 412 Anglican churches dedicated to St Nicolas in England.

By train: Bookham in Surrey.

Polesden Lacey

Great Bookham, nr Dorking, Surrey RH5 6BD

www.nationaltrust.org.uk

The 1400 acre estate, situated on the North Downs, is owned by the National Trust and commands some of the finest views in Surrey. The Edwardian Garden extends to 30 acres with 10 acres of lawns and elegant grass terraces, including a walled rose garden, summer border and winter displays. The house has had a number of famous owners such as the poet and playwright Richard Brinsley Sheridan, who purchased the house in 1804, and Mrs Greville, a legendary Edwardian hostess who extended her hospitality to the Duke and Duchess of York (later to become King George VI and Queen Elizabeth), who spent part of their honeymoon there in 1923.

By road 5ml NW of Dorking, 2ml S of Great Bookham, off A246 Leatherhead-Guildford road.

By train Boxhill & Westhumble 2ml by scenic path through NT park.

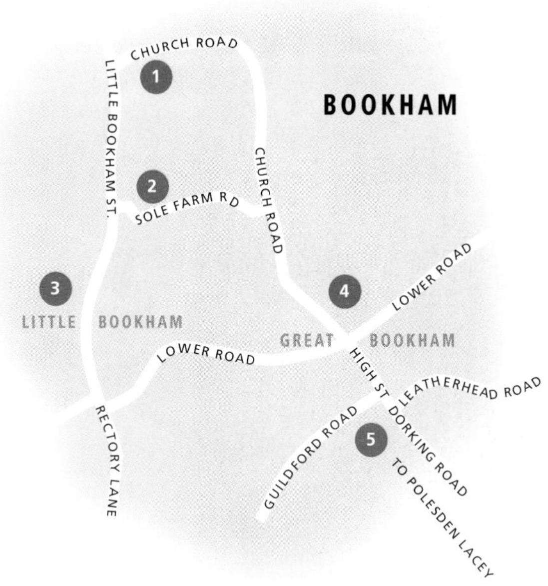

City Cemetery, Falls Road, Belfast

☎ 028 90 320202 ext.3438
www.belfastcity.gov.uk
A Victorian cemetery opened in 1869. The 99 acre site boasts many fine architectural monuments to Belfast's most famous citizens. Members of the Lewis and Hamilton families are buried here. The City Cemetery is located at the junction of Whiterock and Falls Road in west Belfast.

Gladstone's Library, St Deiniol's

Church Lane, Hawarden, Flintshire
☎ 01244 532350
http://www.st-deniolss.org
St Deiniol's Library is Britain's only residential library. Founded by the great Victorian statesman, William Ewart Gladstone (1809–1898), four times Prime Minister of Great Britain and former Chancellor of the Exchequer. Gladstone's original donation of 30,000 books has now grown to around 250,000 items and provides a unique resource for theology and nineteenth century studies.

KEY TO PLACES

1 ROUTE WALKED BY KIRKPATRICK AND LEWIS WHEN LEWIS ARRIVED AT BOOKHAM (LITTLE BOOKHAM STREET WAS UNMADE THEN)

2 SITE OF GASTONS FARMHOUSE (ABOVE) NOTE: THIS IS NOW A PRIVATE RESIDENCE

3 OLD WINDSOR PUBLIC HOUSE

4 ST. NICHOLAS' CHURCH

5 ROAD LAYOUT AS IN 1930—SLIGHTLY CHANGED TODAY

❸ Into battle and beyond

The joy of winning a scholarship at Oxford was tempered by the outbreak of the Great War. Lewis was wounded in action in the Battle of Arras; and the death of a friend and fellow soldier led to an unlikely relationship that would last for more than thirty years

WT Kirkpatrick and Albert Lewis maintained regular contact during Jack's period at Great Bookham, in order to monitor his progress and discuss his proposed future career. Kirkpatrick was in no doubt of Jack's exceptional ability, informing Albert that, 'He was born with the literary temperament and we have to face that fact and all it implies.' They eventually agreed, much to Jack's delight, that he should try for a place at Oxford. On 4 December 1916 CS Lewis sat and won a scholarship to University College.

However, Jack was to remain with Kirkpatrick for another three months while he endeavoured to grasp the rudimentary knowledge of mathematics required to pass 'Responsions'—a necessary formality for entrance to the university. Jack was invited to begin his first term at Oxford on 26 April 1917 and having twice failed the Responsions exam, he had the good fortune to be exempted due to his having joined the Officers' Training Corps as soon as he had arrived at University College. This was particularly fortunate for, in

Above: *The view from CS Lewis' rooms at University College, Oxford in 1919 remains largely unchanged today*

Facing page: *The 'Dreaming Spires' of Oxford*

complete contrast to his mother's aptitude for the subject, he seems to have had a mental block with regard to mathematics, and if the university had not waived the passing of this exam for those in military service he would, in his own words, 'have had to abandon the idea of going to Oxford.'

Jack's father was divided in his feelings towards his son's scholarship. On the one hand he was immensely proud of his achievement, but on the other he was anxious that his enlisting in the services would inevitably expose him to danger. With his son Warren already serving in France, Albert's fears were understandable and he set about, with Kirkpatrick's support, urging Jack to seek an exemption from military service.

According to Albert, Jack was

Above: *Aerial view, Oxford*

Facing page: *University College, Oxford*

Below: *Warren Lewis on leave at Glenmachan in 1915*

eligible, under the Military Service Act, to apply for an exemption on the grounds that he was an Irishman resident in Great Britain for the purpose of his education only. Warnie dismissed his father's argument in favour of getting Jack exempted with the retort, 'If being a Nationalist entitles a man to exemption, what is the reward for a Sinn Féinner? An annuity I suppose!'

Ties that bind

Within his first term at University College in 1917 Jack had enlisted, and by June of that year he had joined a cadet battalion and was moved across Oxford to Keble College which was being used as the Officers' Training Centre. Jack's room-mate was a fellow Irishman, Edward Francis Courtenay Moore, or 'Paddy' as he was commonly known. Paddy had invited Jack to meet his mother who, with her daughter Maureen, had moved from Bristol and taken up residence in Oxford in order to be near her son pending his posting to the Front line. Jack took an instant liking to Mrs Moore and, on Paddy's invitation, spent a week with the family. He informed his father in August of that year: 'I like her immensely and we had a most enjoyable afternoon and evening together.'

Mrs Jane ('Janie') Moore was forty-five at the time she met Jack, who was almost nineteen years old. In 1907 Jane had separated from her husband, Courtenay Edward Moore, and moved to Bristol. Her husband, whom she referred to as 'The Beast', was a graduate of Trinity College,

Dublin, and the son of Canon Courtenay Moore, Rector of Mitchelstown in County Cork, and he worked as a Chief Engineer for Dublin South-Eastern Railways. Jane was born in Pomeroy, County Tyrone, the eldest of three daughters and five sons of the Reverend William James Askins. Her father was a curate in Pomeroy before the family moved to County Louth in 1872 where he took up the position of Vicar of Dunany and Dunleer from 1872 to his death in1895.

It appears that Jack developed an infatuation for Mrs Moore during these visits and it was not long before he was attempting to conceal this relationship from his father. On 25 September Jack was gazetted into the 3rd Somerset Light Infantry and given a month's leave prior to being posted. Albert was hurt, and his suspicions aroused, when Jack decided to spend the first three weeks of a month's leave with the Moore family at their home in Clifton, Bristol, rather than returning immediately to Little Lea. It was during this period that Jack and Paddy Moore pledged that if anything happened to either of them, the survivor would look after the other's parent. It was a promise that was to have a profound effect on the future course of CS Lewis' life.

Jack arrived home in Belfast on the 12 October 1917 for the final week of his leave and it appears relations with his father were strained by what Albert perceived as a slight by his son. Jack confided his amorous feelings for Mrs Moore to Arthur Greeves during this stay and on arriving back in England and discussing the matter with Mrs Moore, regretted this confession. He wrote to Greeves asking him to forget his various statements and never to refer to the subject again, adding 'that topic must be taboo between us.'

Into the trenches

Following his week at Little Lea, Jack crossed over to England and joined his regiment at Crown Hill, near Plymouth. On 15 November 1917, after a forty-eight-hour leave, the 3rd Somerset Light Infantry were to proceed to France. Jack had been commissioned a 2nd Lieutenant with the regiment when, at the last minute, he was suddenly transferred from the 3rd to the 1st Somerset Light Infantry.

Jack sent a telegram to his father informing him of his imminent departure for France and requesting him, due to the short time of the leave, which he would be spending at the home of Mrs Moore in Bristol, to come

Above: *Mrs 'Janie' Moore c. 1908. Mrs Moore first met CS Lewis in 1917 when he was billeted with her son 'Paddy' at Keble College, Oxford*

there to see him off. His father, not understanding the message, wrote back asking him to clarify by letter. Sadly, by the time Albert received Jack's explanatory letter, his son had crossed to France on 17 November 1917. On the day of his nineteenth birthday Jack arrived at the front line trenches. Warnie Lewis, who was also serving with the British Expeditionary Force in France, was promoted to Captain on the same day.

In the event, the danger came from another quarter and Jack

Above: *Keble College, Oxford. The College was designed by the English architect William Butterfield (1814–1900) who was also responsible for designing CS Lewis' local Belfast church of St Mark's, Dundela*

was taken ill with Pyrexia, or 'Trench Fever', and admitted to 10th Red Cross Hospital, Le Treport, on 1 February 1918.

Albert wrote to Warnie informing him that it is 'a cause of heartache and bitter tears' that Jack has been laid up in a military hospital. Warnie saw his father's reaction to Jack's illness as evidence of the unreality of the war to those in Ulster who had not yet been bereaved by it. If any other father in England had received such news, he would have been overjoyed that his son was removed from immediate danger. In Warnie's words, he would have thanked God and gone to his day's work, 'exulting in the news of the safety of his child.'

It appears that Jack's romance with Mrs Moore caused his friend Arthur Greeves some jealousy. However, Lewis placated Arthur, affirmed the strength of their friendship, encouraged Arthur and Mrs Moore to exchange letters, and before long Jack was overjoyed that, 'the two people who matter most to me in the world' are now in correspondence.

Wounded by friendly fire

Following his discharge from the military hospital on the 28

***Above:** The Church of Ireland at Dunany in County Louth. Jane Askins (Mrs Moore) spent her childhood in this area*

Above: A group of Keble College OTC cadets in the summer of 1917, a year before Paddy was killed in action. Jack is the one looking over Paddy Moore's shoulder

Right: CS Lewis stayed in lodgings at 1 Mansfield Road, on his first visit to Oxford in 1916. He recorded his first impression of Oxford: 'The place has surpassed my wildest dreams: I never saw anything so beautiful.'

February, Jack rejoined his battalion at Fampoux before embarking on a four-day tour in the front line of the Battle of Arras in March and again in April. When the great German attack came in the spring of 1918 his regiment experienced heavy shelling, 'about three a minute all day', as the enemy attempted to 'keep them quiet' whilst concentrating their efforts on attacking the Canadians on the right of Jack's unit. Lewis modestly skips over an incident in his autobiography when he 'captured' around sixty German prisoners, by recounting his relief at discovering that 'the crowd of field-grey figures who suddenly appeared from nowhere all had their hands up.' The Great War left no-one who had experienced it unchanged, and Second Lieutenant CS Lewis was no exception: the fear, the smell of high explosive, the barren landscape devoid of even a blade of grass, and the 'horribly smashed men still moving like half-crushed beetles' appeared unreal to him, and the young nineteen year old felt these experiences seemed 'to have happened to someone else.'

CS Lewis was wounded by an English shell during the battle which centred on the village of Riez du Vinage, north-east of Mount Bernenchon, as the allies faced the final German attack on the Western Front. Jack received flesh wounds on the left side of his body—to hand, back of the leg and under the armpit, with a piece of shrapnel entering from behind and ending up lodged in his chest. He was one of the lucky ones: the losses of the 1st Battalion of the Somerset Light Infantry between the 14 and 16 April 1918 were estimated at 210 killed, wounded or missing. His aunt's comment, who was obviously relieved as to the explanation of his injuries, 'Oh, so *that's* why you were wounded in the back!' was one of Lewis' lighter memories of his wartime experiences. Lewis was removed to the various hospitals before being transferred, at his own request, to Ashton Court Hospital, Bristol. He was dejected and homesick when, after being

Mrs Jane Moore

The relationship with Mrs Moore has been well covered by CS Lewis' biographers. George Sayer, who was a friend and former pupil of Lewis' at Magdalen College, revised his earlier opinion and was certain that Lewis and Mrs Moore were lovers. He bases this on later conversations with Mrs Moore's daughter, Maureen, among other considerations. Sayer concludes that it was not a simple relationship of lover and mistress. Jack also thought of her as a mother and she thought of Jack as a substitute for her dead son. According to Mrs Moore's daughter, her father refused to divorce her, so that ruled

out marriage, otherwise Jack and Janie Moore would have married. That they wrote to each other every day in 1919 says something of their closeness. Those who knew CS Lewis are agreed that despite his human failings, he was not a hypocrite. Jack and Paddy had pledged to look after each other's surviving parent should either of them be killed; when Paddy was killed, Lewis honoured his promise. The exact nature of Jack's relationship with Mrs Moore remained obscure even to his closest friends, and the bond which held them together ended only with her death. Whilst Lewis' Christian conversion certainly changed their relationship, it was not a friendship he wished to abandon. Inviting his brother Warren to join them as a permanent member of their household at the Kilns in Oxford in 1930, he was unapologetic for the decision to form a family with the Moores—'I have definitely chosen and I don't regret the choice.'

***Above:** The 10th Red Cross Hospital, Le Treport, France, in 1917 where Lewis recovered from Trench Fever*

***Above:** Insignia of the 3rd Somerset Light Infantry*

back from France for four months, his father still refused to visit him in hospital.

Albert's cautious and methodical nature left him ill disposed towards any change in his routine. Though suffering from bronchitis, he was well aware how this apparent rebuttal might appear to his son. Confiding his position to Warnie, who was repeatedly enquiring if he had yet visited Jack, Albert confessed that he was both sorry and ashamed that he had not visited him, but found the pressures of his work simply too great. His father's failure in arranging to meet Jack before he was posted to France, and the further refusal to visit him in hospital when he was wounded, all helped to exacerbate the rift in relations between them. It is not without significance that Jack now regarded Arthur and Mrs Moore as the two people closest to him, rather than his immediate family. Given these circumstances it is not surprising that Jack chose the hospital in Bristol to recuperate, with Mrs Moore living nearby to offer support and comfort. Jack and Mrs Moore were united, not only by their growing affection for each other, but by the news that her only son, Paddy, had been killed in action.

Above: *Albert Lewis' strict work ethic created tension between himself and Jack*

Below: *Belfast Telegraph Headline. The signing of the Armistice agreement on Monday 11 November 1918 signalled the end of the war. Having been 'demobbed', Jack arrived unexpectedly–and to the great delight of his father and brother–for a family reunion at Little Lea, Belfast, on 27 December*

Back to college

Jack returned to University College, Oxford, in January 1919, to begin the Honour Moderations course in Greek and Latin literature. Within a month of his return he was writing proudly to his father informing him that he had been elected Secretary of a literary club in the College called 'The Martlets'. However, Jack's relationship with Mrs Moore was not something that his father approved of. Since returning to Oxford, Mrs Moore and her daughter Maureen had taken up residence nearby, and an unofficial 'family' was established that was to remain in effect for over thirty years. The nature of the relationship between Jack and Mrs Moore was something that also irritated his brother Warnie. He had it on good account that

Belfast Telegraph

[REGISTERED AT THE G.P.O AS A NEWSPAPER] MONDAY, NOVEMBER 11, 1918. Six Pages. One Penn

BREVITIES.

e death occurred in hospital in Derry on rday from typhus of Mr. Cyril C. ugc, M.A., T.C.D., Professor of Modern guages at M'Crea-Magee College.

EN'S OVERCOATS.—Smart, stylish, and made in such a variety of sizes that we fit at least nine men out of every ten.—RNOCKS, LIMITED. 8 ROYAL NUE.—[Advt.]

TTLE FOR XMAS PHOTOS.—12 HIGH EET, BELFAST, BANGOR, and DERRY.

WANTED—

75,000 worth of Old Gold, Diamond-set s, Brooches, also Platinum and old Gold es from artificial teeth. We are giving ium prices just now.—R. M'DOWELL & LTD., 14 High Street.

GERMANY SURRENDERS.

ARMISTICE SIGNED.

HOSTILITIES CEASE.

THE PRIME MINISTER MAKES THE FOLLOWING ANNOUNCEMENT:—

THE ARMISTICE WAS SIGNED AT

assured, whether the German armistice or not

NEW CHANCELLOR'S

Left: *Anstey Villa, 28 Warneford Road, Oxford. Lewis was sharing this house with Mrs Moore and her daughter Maureen in 1919 and again in 1922. Anstey Villa was favourite of the many houses they stayed in at this period*

Below: *Anstey Villa name plaque*

she was a lady and not a 'loose 'un' as he expected, and this simply added to his perplexity. On the one occasion, when Warren attempted to raise the matter with Jack, he was told, in no uncertain terms, to mind his own business. Arthur Greeves also found the situation bewildering, confiding to Warnie that he did not know what to make of the affair except that Mrs Moore was old enough to be Jack's mother and was in 'poor circumstances.'

The reason for Jack's reluctance to discuss the relationship was partly due to his dependence on his father for an income, which he was now using to supplement the 'family' expenditure; it was also partly due to the necessity of keeping this relationship secret from the university authorities lest his academic career should be jeopardised. Perhaps he also felt a sense of guilt for deceiving his father. The result of this deception was that Jack could not be open with his father and had to maintain an elaborate pretence in case Albert should find out that he was maintaining

WB Yeats (1865–1939) and the occult

WB Yeats was born in Dublin and was one of the most influential poets in modern literature. He is regarded as the driving force behind the Irish Literary Revival movement at the beginning of the twentieth century and also founded the famous Abbey Theatre in Dublin. He was awarded the Nobel Prize for literature in 1923.

CS Lewis had two meetings with WB Yeats in Oxford during March 1921. The meetings were to influence Jack's thought and work and had a greater bearing on his own personal life than was immediately apparent. Jack had cultivated an academic interest in the occult since his schooldays at Malvern. Now he was in the presence of 'a learned and responsible writer' who believed seriously in magic. Jack's attraction towards the occult was a mixture of repulsion and desire, and though secure in his atheism at this point, the conversation with Yeats added weight and lent legitimacy to the idea that there is a world behind, or around, the material world. That the chief advocate for the supernatural should be one of the most revered Irish poets of his age, and a man whose praises Jack had sung for a number of years, merely served to make the idea more alluring. Lewis came to believe in later life that there are no 'accidents' with God and his influential meeting with Yeats reinforced the reality of the idea—that his governess Annie Harper had introduced to his mind as a boy—of an otherworld beyond the world we know.

Left: *Lewis was surprised to learn that Yeats 'believed seriously in Magic'. The physical appearance of the Magician in Dymer is based on CS Lewis' previous meetings with Yeats*

Below: *WB Yeats' house at 4 Broad Street, Oxford. Lewis described how he went up a long staircase lined with pictures by William Blake from the 'Book of Job' and 'Paradise Lost', into a 'very funny room' with 6-ft candlesticks, flame-coloured curtains, a great many pictures, and some strange foreign looking ornaments*

Above: One of the two (east and west) Proctor's Rostra in The Sheldonian Theatre from which CS Lewis read, 'in cap, gown and full evening dress' his prize-wining essay 'Optimism' in 1921

three people instead of one.

It was during this time at University College that Jack's volume of poems *Spirits in Bondage: A Cycle of Lyrics* (written under the pseudonym Clive Hamilton) was published on 20 March 1919. According to Lewis, the common thread throughout is 'that nature is wholly diabolical and malevolent, and that God, if he exists, is outside of and in opposition to the cosmic arrangements.' The correspondence between Albert and Warnie—they had both read the book in manuscript—reveal that they thought Jack declaring his atheism publicly was unnecessary, with Warnie adding, 'that a profession of a Christian belief is as necessary a part of a man's mental make up as a belief in the King, the Regular Army, and the Public Schools.' Albert retained his faith in Jack and, in a comment that does him credit, adds that his son will learn in due course that a man has not solved the mysteries of creation at twenty years of age but, if Oxford does not spoil him, 'he may write something that men would not willingly let die.'

What his father did not realise was that Jack had been having difficulties with his Christian upbringing prior to his confirmation. These adolescent doubts gradually reflected the atheism which persisted throughout Jack's time at Malvern and Great Bookham. That Lewis's first published work should

Below: *58 Windmill Road, Headington, Oxford. Lewis and the Moores lived here in 1920, just a few doors from their previous house Hillview*

Bottom: *Courtfield Cottage, 131 Osler Road, Headington, Oxford. Another temporary home to Lewis and the Moores*

explore these doubts is a natural development of his mental and spiritual position at this time, and is the product of many years of contemplation.

On the 16 July 1923, Lewis received news that he had obtained a First in the English school, adding to his already impressive achievement of a Double First in Classics, and bringing his time at University College to an end. When we consider that since 1919 Jack had been moving from rented accommodation–'most of them vile'–with Mrs Moore and her daughter Maureen, and listing a total of nine different addresses up to 1922 in his diary, we realise just how far he had come from the comfort of Little Lea.

The financial strain was something that Jack had been unaccustomed to at home in Belfast, and the attempts to make

Left: *Hillsboro House, 14 Holyoake Road, Headington, Oxford. CS Lewis and the Moores lived here from 1923 to 1930*

a home for his new 'family' under such circumstances left him: 'in such a rage against poverty and fear and all the infernal net I seem to be in, that I went out and mowed the lawn and cursed all the gods for half an hour…[till] I was tired and sane again.'

The completion of his degrees at University College presented him with the urgent task of securing a job, and as no vacancies were forthcoming, he managed to survive by marking examination papers, giving private tuition, and eventually, securing a temporary post as Philosophy tutor at his old college whilst the current holder was on study leave in America. Jack had hoped to secure a lectureship in Philosophy, but later conceded in a letter to his father that such a vocation was unsuited to the Lewis temperament. He had come to think that whilst he had the mind, he did 'not have the brain and nerves for a life of pure philosophy' with its 'continued search among the abstract roots of things, a perpetual questioning of all that plain men take for granted.' However, whilst Jack might have questioned the usefulness of such philosophical reasoning, he did not suspect just how effective this training would become in his future career as a defender of the Christian faith.

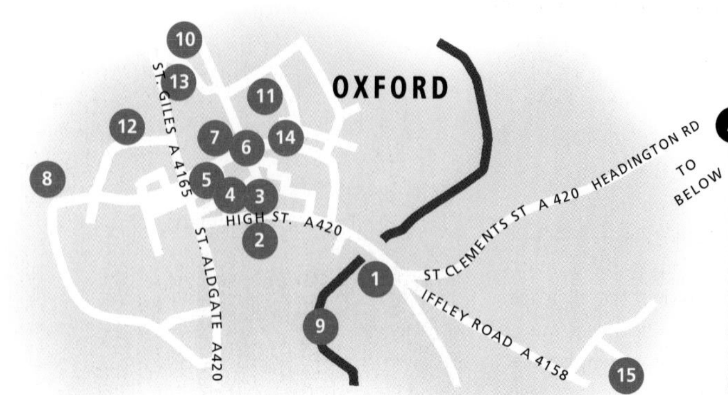

KEY TO PLACES

1 MAGDALEN COLLEGE
2 UNIVERSITY COLLEGE
3 UNIVERSITY CHURCH OF ST MARY THE VIRGIN
4 RADCLIFFE CAMERA
5 BODLEIAN LIBRARY
6 SHELDONIAN THEATRE
7 NEW BODLEIAN LIBRARY
8 ASMOLEAN MUSEUM
9 UNIVERSITY OF OXFORD BOTANIC GARDEN
10 KEBLE COLEGE
11 MANSFIELD COLLEGE
12 EAGLE AND CHILD INN
13 LAMB AND FLAG INN
14 1 MANSFIELD ROAD
15 ANSTEY VILLAS, 28 WARNEFORD ROAD

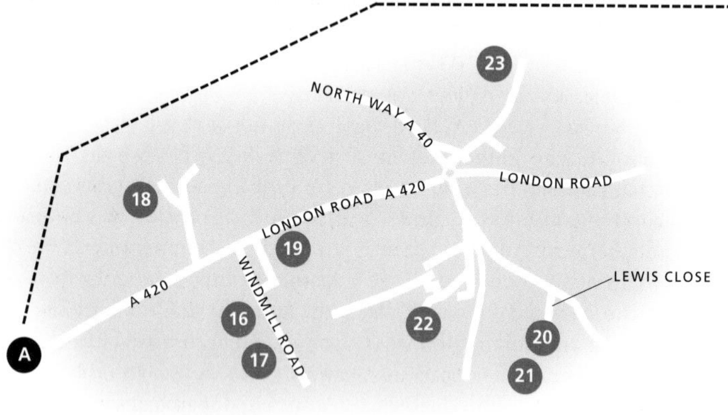

16 58 WINDMILL ROAD, HEADINGTON
17 HILLVIEW, 76 WINDMILL ROAD, HEADINGTON
18 COURTFIELD COTTAGE, 131 OSLER ROAD, HEADINGTON
19 HILLSBORO HOUSE, 14 HOLYOAKE ROAD, HEADINGTON
20 THE KILNS
21 CS LEWIS NATURE RESERVE
22 HOLY TRINITY CHURCH, HEADINGTON QUARRY
23 OXFORD CREMATORIUM

TRAVEL INFORMATION

University College, Oxford

☎ 01865 276602
www.univ.ox.ac.uk
CS Lewis won a scholarship to University College (or 'Univ', as it is known in Oxford) in April 1917. The college was used as an army hospital during the war and Lewis was one of about a dozen other members of 'Univ' who were still in residence there. Following the war, Lewis returned to University College to resume his studies on 13 January 1919.

Sheldonian Theatre

Keble College, Oxford

☎ 01865 272727
www.keble.ox.ac.uk
Keble College was founded in 1870 as a memorial to the Revd John Keble, one of the leaders of the Oxford Movement. Keble, together with Edward Pusey and John Newman, formed the Oxford (or Tractarian) Movement which almost split the Church of England in two. CS Lewis had joined the Officers' Training Corps on his arrival in Oxford in 1917 and was billeted at Keble soon after. His address was: No 738 Cadet CS Lewis, E Company, Keble College, Oxford. Keble College is located off Banbury Road (past St Gilės) on Keble Road and Parks Road.

Keble College

Sheldonian Theatre, Broad Street,Oxford

☎ 01865 277299
http://www.sheldon.ox.ac.uk
The Sheldonian Theatre was erected between 1664–1668 to a design by Sir Christopher Wren. The main purpose of the theatre is to provide the University of Oxford with a place for public meetings and ceremonies. There are also recitals of classical music and other similar events on occasions. The building is of considerable historical and architectural interest. There is a small admission fee.

4 Poet, atheist and Oxford don

For all his academic brilliance CS Lewis had yet to secure permanent employment. He was eking out a living by marking examination papers, giving private tuition, and working as a temporary tutor—when the opening he had always hoped for arrived

Albert Lewis' diary entry for May 1925 expresses the joy he felt on being informed of his son's appointment to a Fellowship in English Language and Literature at Magdalen College, Oxford: 'I went into his room and burst into tears of joy. I knelt down and thanked God with a full heart. My prayers have been heard and answered.' The immediate consequence of the Magdalen appointment was Jack's financial independence from his father, and this led to a lightening in the somewhat tense relationship that existed between them. Albert noted that the fortnight's holiday they spent together 'passed without a cloud.'

One of Lewis' first pupils at Magdalen was the future Poet Laureate, John Betjeman, and within a short time it became clear that the two did not get on. Betjeman's popularity now rests largely on his reputation as a broadcaster, journalist, and critic of architecture (his introduction to *Collins Guide to English Parish Churches* in 1958 is a good example), as much as his standing as a poet. Lewis was exasperated with Betjeman's slack attitude towards his studies. One of

Above: *Magdalen College, Oxford, where CS Lewis was Fellow in English Language and Literature for almost thirty years*

Facing page: *Oxford High Street with Magdalen College Tower in the background*

Top: *Magdalen College lecture at the close of the nineteenth century*

Above: *Cloister in Magdalen College*

Left: *Sir John Betjeman who was one of Lewis's first pupils at Magdalen College*

Betjeman's more dramatic excuses for not handing in an essay on time involved his sudden realisation that he was a failure and would therefore have to abandon his studies and take 'Holy Orders', but being in such an agony of doubt, he could not decide whether he wanted to be 'a very High Church clergyman with a short lacy surplice, or a very Low Church clergyman with long grey moustaches.' Lewis was not impressed, and once described Betjeman as an 'idle prig'. The ill-will was reciprocal: Betjeman was deeply upset at leaving Oxford without a degree and partly blamed his old tutor for this. The effect of this caused him much discomfort in his earlier years and by 1935 he was still annoyed with Lewis, confiding in a letter that, 'I must get him psycho-analysed out of me.'

Academia, atheism and theism

During the period from 1925 to 1930, Lewis settled into the routine of lecturing, tutoring, reading, and writing. He was intellectually stimulated in his studies and teaching, but found himself unsettled in his spiritual life. He was trying to incorporate some of his turbulent experiences during the last decade into a work that was proving difficult to finish successfully. The work dated back to the Christmas holidays of 1916, when he had begun a prose tale called 'Dymer' that was based on an idea that simply came to him of 'a man who, on some mysterious bride, begets a monster: which monster, as soon as it has killed its father, becomes a god.' By the

Left: Detail of a painting of Albert Lewis in 1917 by the artist AR Baker (1865–1939). Baker was born in Southampton and taught at the Government School of Art, Belfast from 1890–1934. He had studios in Royal Avenue, Belfast, not far from Albert Lewis' legal practice

time *Dymer* was published in September 1926, Jack's atheistic outlook was beginning to waver. Lamenting the 'unholy muddle' he was in regarding the imagination and the intellect, he was forced to confront what exactly he did believe. In the midst of this uncertainty, an unexpected event was to mark yet another defining moment in Lewis' spiritual odyssey.

Albert Lewis was suffering from acute abdominal cramps during the summer months of 1929 and on the advice of Jack's cousin, Joey Lewis, who was a consultant physician and bacteriologist at the Belfast Infirmary, it was decided that he should be sent for X-rays to determine the cause. The tests were inconclusive and an exploratory operation was conducted and revealed, what everyone had feared, that Albert had cancer.

Jack had arrived at Little Lea on the 13 August and had been nursing his father, often in terrible agony, throughout this period. But as the doctors concluded that Albert had every possibility of living for a number of years, Jack decided to return to Oxford to tackle the ever increasing backlog of work that had accumulated in his absence. He arrived at Magdalen College on the 22 September only to receive a telegram on the 25th announcing that his father had taken a turn for the worse. He left immediately and arrived in Belfast the next morning to discover that his father had died on the afternoon of the previous day.

Even while nursing his father through his illness, Jack had found himself still torn between duty and disgruntlement towards his father. A fortnight before Albert's death he wrote to his friend Owen Barfield of his attending the almost painless sickbed of 'one for whom I have little affection and whose society has for many years given me much discomfort and no pleasure' and musing on 'what in heaven's name must it be like to fill the same place at the sickbed, perhaps agonised, of someone really loved, and someone whose loss will be irreparable?' Little did CS Lewis know that one day he was to discover the answer to this question in nursing his terminally ill wife.

Following his father's death, Lewis underwent a spiritual rebirth. The tentative steps he was taking towards a full acceptance of Christianity over the last few years were now leading him on a path for which he had been searching since childhood. Jack's journey from atheism to Christianity occurred over a number of years and is recorded in depth in his spiritual autobiography *Surprised by Joy*.

The vague stirrings of what he was later to term *joy*, first surfaced when Warnie presented him with that toy garden when they were children at Dundela Villas, and which triggered in him an intense longing for something that he could not define. He knew only that this desire was 'an unsatisfied desire which is itself

Above: *St Mark's Church as seen from the site of where Dundela Villa used to stand*

Above: *To the young CS Lewis, Little Lea 'seemed less like a house than a city'*

Below: *The Blue Plaque marking CS Lewis' time at Little Lea*

more desirable than any other satisfaction' and that anyone who had experienced it will want it again. The importance of this concept of joy cannot be overestimated; he readily admitted, 'in a sense the central story of my life is about nothing else.' The longing for a form to express this desire proved elusive.

Early in 1926 an event had occurred, coinciding with the publication of *Dymer*, that had an alarming effect on Jack. His arguments for rejecting Christianity were being subjected to systematic spiritual erosion, beginning when one of 'the hardest boiled of all atheists I ever knew' sat in his rooms at Magdalen College and announced that the evidence for the historicity of the Gospels was really surprisingly good. This revelation, coming shortly after his reading of GK Chesterton's *Everlasting Man*, was another push towards an acceptance of Christ. Up to this point, Lewis had been an avid reader of Chesterton and thought him the most sensible man alive—'apart from his Christianity.' In reading George MacDonald and Chesterton, Lewis admits he did not know what he was letting himself in for, adding, 'a young man who wishes to remain a sound Atheist cannot be too careful of his reading.'

Another defining moment in the life of the Lewis brothers occurred when they visited their childhood home of Little Lea for the last time during April 1930. Following the death of his father, Jack and Mrs Moore had travelled to Belfast the previous year to clear out Little Lea in preparation

Warren Hamilton ('Warnie') Lewis (1895–1973)

CS Lewis once described his older brother 'Warnie' as his 'dearest and closest friend' and the two were inseparable, living together most of their lives. Warnie was a career army officer who had been prepared for the Sandhurst entrance examination by Jack's tutor, WT Kirkpatrick. He served as an officer with the Royal Army Service Corps and during the First World War served in France and later in Sierra Leone, West Africa. Whilst stationed in Shanghai, China, he had a profound reawakening of his Christian faith whilst gazing at the Great Buddha of Kamakura in May 1930. He later recorded in his diary that this experience was no sudden impulse but, much like that of his brother Jack, the result of a growing conviction of the truth of Christianity. He described his faith as a wheel which had made the full revolution from 'indifference, scepticism, atheism, agnosticism, and back again to Christianity.'

He was an industrious and highly civilised man who wrote seven books on seventeenth and eighteenth century France. Unfortunately, his father's advice to Warnie on his posting to France to 'have little or nothing to do with vin—either ordinaire or particular' was sadly to become only too relevant in Warnie's case. He suffered a lifelong struggle with alcoholism.

Pictured: *Warren (right) and 'Jack' in 1920*

Above: *Jack and Warnie loved to cycle in the countryside around Belfast. They remained the closest of friends throughout their lives*

for the sale of the property.

Warnie provides a poignant account of himself and Jack clearing out their old home and taking turns digging a hole in the garden in which to bury their childhood hoard of stuffed animals and china figures, which were characters in their created imaginary world of Boxen. Warnie found the final parting with Little Lea 'beastly' and the thought 'that one would never again crunch down the gravel drive...on the way to the boat' marked yet another wrench in the history of the Lewis family. No longer is Little Lea viewed as the family home: 'The house has been well suffered in' was Jack's observation, and in his poem, 'Leaving Forever the Home of One's Youth', he laid the ghosts of Leeborough to rest:

Drive on and look not out.
Though from each tree
Grey memories drop and
dreams thick-dusted lie
Beneath; though every other
place must be
Raw, new, colonial country
till we die.

The Kilns

The Kilns

The question of where Warnie was now to call home was resolved when he, Jack and Mrs Moore pooled their resources from the sale of Little Lea and bought their own home, the Kilns in Headington Quarry, Oxford. On 11 October 1930 they, together with Mrs Moore's daughter Maureen, moved in. The house was set in more than eight acres and took its name from the remains of two old brick-kilns which stood on the site. There were also gardens, a tennis court, greenhouse, and a small lake

George MacDonald (1824–1905)

The Scottish poet, preacher, and lecturer, was one of the most important influences on CS Lewis. MacDonald was the son of a Scottish weaver and trained as a Congregational minister. He was a friend of John Ruskin, the famous art critic, poet, artist, writer and social reformer, and also of the author of *Alice in Wonderland*, Lewis Carroll. MacDonald has maintained a solid reputation as a writer of fantasy and children's literature. Lewis described how his own imagination, was in a sense, 'baptised' on first reading MacDonald's novel *Phantastes.* Lewis openly acknowledged MacDonald as his 'master' and that it was in his works that he first met the quality of 'holiness.'

The debt that Lewis owed MacDonald is indicated in his claim that he had 'never written a book in which I did not quote from him.' MacDonald even appears as his 'spiritual guide' in Lewis' fantasy novel *The Great Divorce.* MacDonald's 'universalism' (the belief which includes the idea that all mankind will be saved and that hell is not everlasting) was something that Lewis did not agree with, and he explained in some detail his objections to it in the eighth chapter of his book *The Problem of Pain.* Lewis alluded to his disagreement with his master in the preface to *George MacDonald: An Anthology*, but went on to add that he knew of hardly any other writer who 'seems closer, or more continually close, to the Spirit of Jesus Himself.'

***Above:** 'Shelley's Pool,' once in the grounds of the Kilns, now part of the CS Lewis Nature Reserve. Lewis once received a pair of breeding swans from the Provost of Worcester College, which he enjoyed feeding* ***Below:** The Kilns wall plaque*

known locally as 'Shelley's Pool', where it is reputed that the Romantic poet Shelley used to meditate.

The purchase of the Kilns gave Jack a sense of peace and stability and it was to remain his home for the rest of his life. Writing about the house to Arthur Greeves, Jack enthused, 'But oh!—I never hoped for the like.'

Warnie saw his brother's Christian conversion as no 'sudden plunge into a new life, but rather a slow steady convalescence from a deep-seated spiritual illness of long standing.' It is Jack's intimate experience of the 'spiritual illness' of unbelief over such a long period that gives his post-conversion writings such force and insight, and goes some way towards explaining his popular appeal as an 'apostle to the skeptics.' Readers of his theological works find many of their doubts, not only raised, but convincingly answered by Lewis. This was also something of a gestation period, as far as thoughts and feelings about God were concerned, and by the early 1930s, he was compelled to face up to what exactly he did believe regarding the Person of Jesus Christ.

The Ashmolean Museum of Art

TRAVEL INFORMATION

Magdalen College, High Street, Oxford

☎ 01865 276000
www.magd.ox.ac.uk

Founded as Magdalen Hall by William Waynflete, Bishop of Winchester and Lord Chancellor of England, in 1448. It became Magdalen College (pronounced 'Maudlin') in 1458. The tradition of the singing of a hymn on top of the Tower at dawn on May Day morning is still alive and featured in Richard Attenborough's film of CS Lewis' life, *Shadowlands*.

The Ashmolean Museum of Art and Archaeology

Beaumont Street, Oxford
☎ 01865 278000
www.magd.ox.ac.uk

Founded in 1683, the Ashmolean has the distinction of being Britain's oldest public museum. A rich and diverse collection of British, European, Egyptian and Near Eastern antiquities is on display including: European paintings and drawings, sculpture, silver, ceramics, musical instruments and coins and medals.

University of Oxford Botanic Garden, Rose Lane, Oxford

☎ 01865 286690
http://www.botanic-garden.ox.ac.uk

The oldest botanic garden in England, founded in 1621, boasting over 150 species of trees and over 8,000 varieties of plants. There is a rock garden, water garden, and several glasshouses, and a wonderful view of Magdalen Tower from the garden; the garden is opposite Magdalen College.

The Henry Stephens C. S. Lewis Reserve Local Wildlife Trust

Lewis Close, Headington, Oxford.

This 'nature reserve' is owned by the Berkshire, Buckinghamshire and Oxfordshire Wildlife Trust and was once part of CS Lewis' garden at the Kilns. There is a path leading into the reserve at the top of Lewis Close.

The Kilns, Lewis Close, Headington, Oxford, OX3 8JD UK

www.cslewis.org

The Kilns is now owned by the CS Lewis Foundation of Redlands, California, and functions as a home for graduate students of Oxford University and as a Christian study centre, with regular summer seminars. Tours of the home are conducted by appointment only.

☎ 01865–741865

Top: *The Kilns*

Middle: *The Living Room of The Kilns*

Bottom: *CS Lewis' bedroom at The Kilns*

5 The pilgrim awakes

CS Lewis's atheistic philosophy crumbled as he finally submitted to God. He recounted his Christian conversion in his first major prose work, *The Pilgrim's Regress*

CS Lewis has described how, during the Trinity term of 1929, God 'closed in' on him and how he felt the unrelenting approach of God as he sat, night after night, in his rooms at Magdalen College. Realising that total surrender was required, Lewis at last gave in, knelt down in his room and prayed. As he wrote later, 'I was to be allowed to play at philosophy no longer.' He acknowledged 'that God was God' and went to bed that night 'the most dejected and reluctant convert in all England.'

However, this conversion was to theism only–the belief that there is a God–and it was not until October 1931 that he could finally announce to Arthur Greeves that he had just passed from believing in God, to definitely believing in Christ and Christianity. Jack was still plagued with doubts about what Christian doctrine, and in particular the doctrine of Redemption, actually meant. In reconsidering his earlier enthusiastic letter to Arthur Greeves on his conversion to Christianity, Jack thought he had been too hasty in affirming his new found belief. He conceded that whilst he had certainly moved a bit, he confessed that he still had difficulties with the phrases he had so often ridiculed in the past,

Above: *The New Building at Magdalen College was built in 1733. CS Lewis, the poet John Betjeman, the historian Edward Gibbon and the essayist, poet and playwright, Joseph Addison, all had their rooms in this building*

Facing page: *Addison's Walk in the grounds of Magdalen College, where CS Lewis' long night talk on 19 September 1931 with fellow Inklings Hugo Dyson and JRR Tolkien, moved him from a belief in God to 'definitely believing in Christ'*

such as 'sacrifice' and 'the blood of the lamb'; phrases he could only interpret in senses that seemed either 'silly or shocking'. In this Lewis was echoing the initial reaction of many new converts to the Christian faith. Behind these conflicting emotions, the work of the Holy Spirit was preparing him for the final step towards Christ.

From Christianity to Christ

Lewis first met Hugo Dyson in his rooms at Magdalen College in July 1930. Dyson was, in Lewis' words, 'a philosopher and a religious man.' He was a practising member of the Church of England—a man who 'really loves truth...none of your damned dilettante.' The two hit it off immediately. Realising that 'such things come rarely,' Lewis recorded that 'we sat up so late with the feeling that heaven knew when we might meet again and the new friendship had to be freed to pass its youth into maturity in a single evening.' This meeting was of more significance than Lewis then realised.

It was not until the following year, 19 September 1931, that they met again. One particular late-night conversation with Hugo Dyson and JRR Tolkien changed CS Lewis' life for ever. They succeeded in helping to remove a stumbling block towards an acceptance of Christ which had been plaguing Lewis for some time.

Above: *Magdalen College deer park. Lewis' rooms in Magdalen College, looked north into the deer park. He wrote to his father, 'my external surroundings are beautiful beyond expectation or hope'*

Strolling in Addison's Walk, in the grounds of Magdalen College, Tolkien pointed out to Lewis that the idea of sacrifice in a pagan story apparently appealed to him if he met it anywhere except in the Gospels. The reason, he explained, was that in pagan stories Jack was prepared to feel the myth as profound and suggestive of meanings that were beyond his grasp, even though he could not describe what it meant in a literal sense, whereas in the Christian message Lewis found that 'a man can accept what Christ has done without knowing how it works.' In the course of the conversation Lewis gradually came to understand the story of Christ as 'a true myth': a myth which works on the imagination in the same way as the others, but with the crucial difference that *it actually happened*. Lewis came to

Above: *Holy Trinity Church at Headington Quarry, where, on Christmas Day 1931, Jack took his first communion since childhood*

understand that the essential thing was 'to accept that which Christ accomplished on the cross.'

However, the urge 'to call one's soul one's own' was still preventing him from taking the next logical step—Clive Staples Lewis still wanted to be in charge of his own destiny. The final barrier was removed during a decidedly undramatic trip to Whipsnade Zoo in the sidecar of Warnie's motorbike on the 28 September 1931! When they set out, Jack did not believe that Jesus Christ was the Son of God and when they reached the zoo he did. For all his intellectual theorising the final step towards Christ was as simple and as uneventful as that. He likened the experience to a man who, after a long sleep and whilst still lying motionless in his bed, becomes aware that he is awake.

On Christmas Day 1931 he made the necessary 'leap of faith' required to move from philosophical reasoning to spiritual commitment, and attended his first Communion since childhood in his parish church at Headington Quarry, Oxford. CS Lewis was now

BORN 1898, REBORN 1931

***Above:** Part of the banner from the foot of The Searcher sculpture*

not only mentally, but spiritually awake.

Lewis now attempted to tell the central story of his own life, the experience of Joy, which had so far eluded him. During a fortnight's holiday at Arthur Greeves' home in Belfast, he wrote the story of his conversion. The book carried the rather academic title of *The Pilgrim's Regress: An Allegorical Apology for Christianity, Reason and Romanticism*. Like *Dymer*, this book saw Jack laying to rest many of his past spiritual and intellectual illusions.

The career of an author

Lewis had been working on another book, *The Allegory of Love*, which charts the history of allegorical love literature from the early Middle Ages to the late sixteenth century, when the inspiration for *The Pilgrim's Regress* came to him. The influence of Bunyan, not only on the title but the form and story of *The Pilgrim's Regress,* is now made explicit and marks the beginning of a story that had preoccupied Jack since his teenage years in Belfast, and was to take over a decade to complete successfully. Like his fictional pilgrim John, Jack Lewis was to return to the Christianity of his childhood, but unlike John, it was to a Christianity that is 'the same yet different': a belief that is

***Left:** 'Bernagh' The home of Lewis' closest friend and lifelong correspondent, Arthur Greeves, was situated just across the road from Little Lea. The house was in later years a nursing home named 'Red Hall' and was demolished in 2003*

utterly transformed and rejuvenated by his personal experience of conversion to Christ.

The Ulsterior Motive?

The significance of the title of *The Pilgrim's Regress* was not lost on Jack's friend, Tolkien, who observed, with some disdain, that the title of the book betrayed not so much a reawakening of the Christian faith of Lewis' childhood, but 'the prejudices so sedulously planted in boyhood'. It is unlikely that Tolkien's condescending remark that Jack 'would become again a Northern Ireland Protestant' was a tribute to the reformed Christian faith which Lewis was raised in and sheds

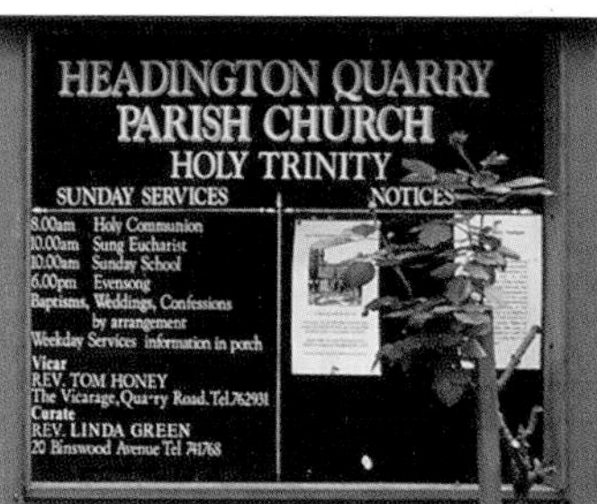

Above: *The notice board of Holy Trinity Church at Headington Quarry*

Top: *Interior of Holy Trinity Church, Headington where, on Christmas Day 1931, CS Lewis attended his first Communion after his conversion*

some light on Tolkien's bias. The title of Tolkien's unpublished essay on Lewis, 'The Ulsterior Motive', would appear to support such an interpretation. The 1964 essay originated as a critique of Lewis' book on prayer, *Letters to Malcolm*. Tolkien found the book 'a distressing and in parts horrifying work', and he realised that if he finished the essay, it would not be publishable. The work remains inaccessible to researchers by the Tolkien estate.

Tolkien's hostility towards Protestantism needs some explanation here. He appears to have been particularly sensitive to any hint of anti-Roman Catholic bias, whether real or imagined, partly as a result of the way his mother was treated by her Protestant relatives when she converted to Roman Catholicism. Later, in the preface to perhaps his greatest work of Christian

The Pilgrim's Regress

The Pilgrim's Regress is the allegorical story of CS Lewis' spiritual journey as told through the central 'Everyman' character of 'John' as he winds his way from illusion to self-knowledge. Lewis has described the concept of Joy as being the central story of his life, and took great pains in various writings to articulate the experience. As John Bunyan, the seventeenth century Puritan Baptist and popular writer, used allegory to show a Christian's journey through the world in his book *The Pilgrim's Progress* (see *Travel with John Bunyan* in this series), Lewis likewise makes good use of this literary form. In *The Pilgrim's Regress* Lewis skilfully details and systematically attacks many of the intellectual, emotional, and political movements of the period—Freudianism, Modernism, Marxism, Humanism, even Anglo-Catholicism, among others, came under his intellectual lash.

The Pilgrim's Regress is a landmark work in Lewis' writings coming as it does at the beginning of his Christian life. It is the first book where we can detect the beginnings of what we would later recognise as CS Lewis' distinctive voice. There is a growing confidence and authority born out of experience as he recounts the intellectual and spiritual travels which led him, 'on the road rarely trodden from popular Realism to philosophical Idealism; from Idealism to Pantheism; from Pantheism to Theism; and from Theism to Christianity'. This is also the first work published under his own name rather than an assumed name. It also marks not just his first work as an avowed 'Christian', but also sees Lewis adopting for the first time the mantle of 'Christian apologist'—his career as a writer now began in earnest.

apologetics, *Mere Christianity*, CS Lewis attempts to explain and defend the beliefs that have been 'common to nearly all Christians at all times' and there is an allusion to the denominational difference with Tolkien. Jack observes that there is no controversy between Christians which needs to be so delicately touched as the attendant Roman Catholic beliefs surrounding the Virgin Birth and how 'it is very difficult so to dissent from them that you will not appear to them a cad as well as a heretic.' Lewis' avoidance of any discussion on the doctrine, peculiar to Roman Catholicism, of the Immaculate Conception which he alluded to in *Mere Christianity*, was an attempt to avoid controversy in a book which was designed to defend 'the belief that has been nearly common to all Christians at all times.'

This is not to suggest that Lewis was unafraid of expressing views which were contrary to those of his academic friends, many of whom were Anglo-Catholic or Catholic. On one occasion Lewis read a paper which critiqued Mariolatry to a regular group who gathered in rooms in Oxford and which comprised Anglicans, Roman Catholics, and Greek and Russian Orthodox believers. The sole Evangelical present records how a number of the group 'really jumped on him' after he finished his talk on Mariolatry and how Lewis, whom, he observed, loved to be outnumbered, robustly defended his views.

However, it must be said that when it came to being sensitive about one's own religion, Lewis was as quick to react as Tolkien was to any supposed slur on his faith. When *The Pilgrim's Regress* was eventually published, Lewis dedicated the work to his friend Arthur Greeves and complained that he was uncomfortable having his book, 'especially a religious book', brought out by a 'Papist publisher' (Sheed and Ward), but as they thought they could sell his book, whereas another publisher thought it might be difficult, Lewis gave in. He told Greeves he had

Above: *Bust of CS Lewis sculpted in 1980 by Faith Tolkien (for a time daughter in law of JRR Tolkien)*

Pictured: *'Tolkien came back with me to college and sat discoursing of the gods and giants of Asgard for three hours', was how Lewis described a typical meeting with his friend during 1929*

JRR Tolkien (1892–1973)

Tolkien first met CS Lewis in May 1926, when Lewis had just been elected tutor at Magdalen College. Tolkien was Rawlinson and Bosworth Professor of Anglo-Saxon at Oxford. Among Lewis' first impressions of Tolkien were that he was 'a smooth, pale, fluent little chap' who thought that 'all literature was for the amusement of men between thirty and forty.' Lewis concluded with: 'No harm in him: only needs a smack or so.' Since his boyhood, Lewis had been 'implicitly warned never to trust a Papist' and on entering the English faculty at Magdalen, explicitly 'never to trust a philologist.' However, finding that Tolkien was both did not hinder a friendship developing between them.

Tolkien had shown Lewis the draft manuscript for *The Hobbit* in 1933, and Lewis was unstinting in his praise for it. Tolkien valued CS Lewis' encouragement and paid tribute to his support and friendship over the twelve years in which he laboured on *The Lord of the Rings,* and that 'but for his interest and unceasing eagerness for more I should never have brought *The Lord of the Rings* to a conclusion.' The book is dedicated to the Inklings, the literary group of which both were members. The relationship between Lewis and Tolkien cooled in later years. Lewis' invitation to his friend, the author and poet, Charles Williams to join the regular Inklings meetings created some friction with Tolkien. The relationship suffered further when he heard, some time after the event, that CS Lewis had married Joy Gresham.

Right: *St. Mark's Church, Dundela, Belfast*

been 'well punished' for his choice of publishers as Sheed and Ward had inserted a blurb on the dust jacket which had stated that 'the story begins in Puritania (Mr Lewis was brought up in Ulster)'. By stressing CS Lewis' Protestant background and its natural affinity with the beliefs of the Puritans, the publisher was implying, Lewis thought, that *The Pilgrim's Regress* was an attack on his Protestant heritage. Lewis urged Greeves that if he ever came across anyone who might be interested, he was to explain as loudly as he could that he was not consulted and that the blurb was 'a damnable lie told to try and make Dublin riff-raff buy the book.'

Lewis was moved and extremely grateful for the warm words of encouragement he received from the Reformed and evangelical preacher, Dr Martyn Lloyd-Jones (1899–1981), when the early edition of *The Pilgrim's Regress* was not selling particularly well. The two met again, on a ferry crossing to Ireland in 1953, and Lewis' response to the Doctor's question of when he would write another book was, 'When I understand the meaning of prayer'. The work on prayer which eventually appeared, gave Lewis some difficulties and

***Left:** The Lewis brothers arrived at St. Mark's Church, Dundela, Belfast, on 8 August 1933 to view the stained glass window which they had commissioned in memory of their parents*

he did not finish it until six months before he died. The posthumous *Letters to Malcolm: Chiefly on Prayer* was published in 1964. It should be added that whilst Lloyd-Jones was on friendly terms with Lewis, he did not accept some of his more imaginative speculations on issues surrounding certain Christian doctrines.

It is clear that Lewis underwent a creative and spiritual rebirth at this point and it is only following *The Pilgrim's Regress* that he went on to develop his own distinctive voice. We see the beginnings of his career as a Christian 'apologist.' In the thirty years following Lewis' conversion, over thirty books were published. Academic works, the *Narnian Chronicles*, Christian apologetics, a space trilogy, a novel, numerous articles, reviews, and letters all flowed from his pen during a sustained period of inspiration.

***Below:** The Latin inscription below the window reads, 'To the greater glory of God and dedicated to the memory of Albert James Lewis, who died on the 25th September 1929, aged 67, and also of his wife Flora Augusta Hamilton, who died on the 23rd August 1908, aged 47*

TRAVEL INFORMATION

Holy Trinity Church, Headington Quarry, Oxford

www.headington.org.uk
☎ 01865 762931
The church, founded in 1848, celebrated its 150th anniversary in 1999 and was designed by Sir Gilbert Scott. CS Lewis and his brother Warren were members of Holy Trinity Church for over thirty years and both are buried in a single grave in the churchyard. Headington Quarry is situated just inside the city ring road, a short distance from the Headington A40 roundabout, some 2.5 miles from Oxford city centre. If approaching by car use Trinity Road (located just off the Headington to Cowley section of the ring road) which runs down to the side of the Six Bells Public House. Visitors can also approach by foot using the narrow lane (Church signposted) from Quarry Road (Margaret Road end).

Above: *The Trout Inn at the village of Godstow on the outskirts of Oxford was a favourite of CS Lewis and his friends in the Inklings*

The Bodleian Library, Broad Street, Oxford

www.bodley.ox.ac.uk
☎ 01865 277000
One of the oldest libraries in the world and the second largest library in Britain. The Bodleian is home to one of the two largest collections of CS Lewis' manuscripts (the other is at the Wade Centre, Wheaton College, USA). Lewis claimed the Bodleian was 'one of the most delightful places in the world' and mentioned studying in 'Duke Humphrey's Library' whilst savouring the atmosphere.

Bodleian Library

The Trout 195 Godstow Road, Lower Wolvercote, Oxford

☎ 01865 302071
Originally a sixteenth century fisherman's house and serving as an inn since 1625. A favourite stopping place for Lewis and his friends in the Inklings.

Whipsnade Wild Animal Park, Dunstable, Bedfordshire

www.whipsnade.co.uk
☎ 01582 872171
Lewis visited here on a number of occasions when it was known as Whipsnade Zoo. It was on the way to Whipsnade in his brother's sidecar that Lewis took the 'final step' of his Christian conversion.

6 The power of the pen

CS Lewis' reputation as a scholar, broadcaster, and increasingly as an outspoken Christian and 'Apostle to the Skeptics', made him a household name on both sides of the Atlantic. In 1947 he appeared on the cover of the American *Time* magazine. However, in robustly defending his Christian faith, Lewis aroused the contempt and intellectual wrath of many in Oxford

CS Lewis' conversion to Christ was the single greatest influence on his life: from this point on, his academic and literary work flourished as he put his spiritual, mental and intellectual life in order. For over a decade he had struggled to fulfil worldly ambitions, first as a poet and later as a philosopher, but now he found the stability, from within and without, to build a solid foundation for his life as a Christian, Oxford don, and writer. The reasonably settled domestic life of Lewis at the Kilns with Mrs Moore, her daughter Maureen, and his brother Warren all led him to declare that 'we make a very contented family together.' Lewis was once asked if the quiet routine of his life was not monotonous; Jack's retort, 'I like monotony', not only baffled the enquirer, but revealed something of Lewis' innate domestic temperament.

His Christian conversion had another remarkable effect on Lewis, in that his literary and scholarly output increased dramatically. There would be no more of the years spent labouring

Above: *The Kilns provided Lewis with the domestic comfort that he longed for*

Facing page: *The pulpit of The University Church of St Mary the Virgin in Oxford where Lewis preached his wartime sermon 'The Weight of Glory'*

on poetry with scant artistic or critical success to show for his efforts. *The Allegory of Love*, together with his other academic works, secured his reputation within Oxford and beyond as a literary historian of the highest order.

In order to write the volume on 'English Literature in the Sixteenth Century', which excluded Drama, in the *Oxford History of English Literature* series in 1954, Lewis set himself the task of reading the *entire works* of about two hundred authors and, in the section of the book dealing with 'Religious Controversy and Translation', he read the complete works of Thomas More, Martin Luther, John Calvin, William Tyndale, John Foxe, and Thomas Cranmer, among many others. Having worked on this for nearly ten years, towards the end his enthusiasm flagged and he confided to a friend that he longed

The Inklings

In the mid 1930s CS Lewis became the centre of an informal group of friends, many of them Christians, who met in his rooms at Magdalen College on Thursday evenings, and later at the Eagle and Child public house (or 'The Bird and Baby' as it was commonly known) in Oxford. They met on Tuesday mornings to read and discuss their work and the group adopted the name 'The Inklings' from an undergraduate literary society which had once existed at University College, Oxford. The name was attractive in its suggestion of people with vague or half-formed ideas coupled with that of 'those who dabble in ink.'

The main thrust of the group was to read and criticise each other's work in progress. This was no mutual admiration society: criticism was frank, but good natured, and the task of reading one's work to such a cultured and literate audience could be daunting. The number of participants varied over the years, but they included his brother Warnie, JRR Tolkien, Hugo Dyson, Owen Barfield and Charles Williams. It was at these meetings that Lewis read *Perelandra, The Great Divorce, The Problem of Pain, Miracles,* and *That Hideous Strength.* The group was in existence until the end of the 1940s when, for a variety of reasons, enthusiasm for the gatherings ran out. The last Thursday meeting of the Inklings was on Thursday 20 October 1949 and the following week Jack's brother Warnie unwittingly recorded the demise of the group in his diary entry: ' No one turned up …'

Pictured: *The Eagle and Child (or 'Bird and Baby') public house where The Inklings met from the mid-thirties to the end of the nineteen forties*

Above: The Radcliffe Camera as seen from St Mary the Virgin—the University Church

to 'turn away from this critical nonsense and write something really worthwhile—theology and fantasy.'

Larger worlds

Lamenting that there was too little of what Lewis and his friend JRR Tolkien liked in stories, they made a bargain to 'write some ourselves'—Tolkien a 'time–journey' and Lewis a 'space-journey', Tolkien began work on the first instalment of 'The Lost Road', which was rejected by his publishers, whilst Lewis finally saw his book *Out of the Silent Planet* published in the autumn of 1938. *Out of the Silent Planet* is Lewis's attack on what he called 'scientism', a belief that the supreme moral end of mankind is the perpetuation of the species regardless of the moral or ethical consequences. The hidden Christian symbolism is evident in

Out of the Silent Planet. The forces behind, and working through, the characters of Ransom and his antagonist Weston, represent God and Satan. The quarrel between these two agencies come into direct conflict in Perelandra in the second book of the trilogy *Perelandra* where Ransom and Weston engage in mortal combat to avert the 'Fall of Man.'

Some idea of Lewis' productivity during this period can be gauged from the fact that between the publication of *Out of the Silent Planet* in 1938 and its sequel *Perelandra* in 1943, there appeared another eight books by Lewis. Many of the major themes

The inspiration of walking tours

Between April 1927 and January 1931, Lewis engaged in no less than five separate walking tours with Oxford friends or his brother Warnie. These walking tours were an important part of his year. The group of friends would set off on a planned route and travel on foot, making stops at village inns on the way for refreshments and lodgings. They usually managed to cover up to twenty miles a day and on the way they indulged in imaginative speculation, conversation, foolery, and an appreciation of the variety of the English countryside. The essence and attraction of the walking tour lies in its simplicity. One has only to consider the fundamentals: food, shelter, and reaching the next destination on the map. For Jack, the joy felt after a day's walking, perhaps in extreme weather, and the relief of spying the lights of a village in the distance where you will spend the night, 'fixes itself in your mind—for enjoyment ten, twenty, or thirty years hence—as a place of impossible peace and dreaminess.'

The walking tours also supply a rich stock of images that embellish, and often find their way into, Lewis' fiction. The first book of his science fiction trilogy, *Out of the Silent Planet*, opens with Dr Elwin Ransom, a middle-aged philologist of Cambridge University, on a walking tour of the English Midlands. Likewise, John's journey in *The Pilgrim's Regress* is basically a spiritual walking tour embedded in the form of an allegory.

Pictured: *The hills above Caergwrle and Hope in North Wales*

Above: The village of Carlingford at the foot of the Cooley Mountains, in the Republic of Ireland. Lewis knew this area well and described the area of County Louth as being 'as near heaven you can get in Thulcandra' (the name he gave to earth in his science fiction trilogy)

and ideas in these works emerge, in one form or another, in the second book of the space trilogy, *Perelandra*. The origins of the second book in the trilogy can be found in a letter to Arthur Greeves in December 1941. Lewis writes that he is engaged on a sequel to *Out of the Silent Planet* in which Ransom now goes to Venus (which is at the Adam-and-Eve stage and the first two rational creatures have just appeared and are still innocent). The hero arrives in time to prevent their 'falling' as *our* first pair did. *Perelandra* is an imaginative reworking of the biblical Fall—a speculative 'Paradise Retained.' The final book in the trilogy, *That Hideous Strength: A Modern Fairy-Tale for Grown-Ups,* brings the cosmic battle between good and evil to earth.

The Screwtape Letters

Lewis conceived the idea for one of his most popular books in July 1940 whilst sitting in his pew during his regular attendance at Holy Trinity Church, Headington Quarry, Oxford. Before the Communion service was over, Lewis was struck with the idea for a book which would be based on letters from an elderly retired devil, Screwtape, to a young and inexperienced apprentice devil. *The Screwtape Letters* originally appeared as a series of thirty-one letters in *The Guardian* during 1941 before appearing as a book the following year. *The Screwtape Letters* and its sequel *Screwtape Proposes a Toast* (1959) were written in the form of epistles or letters, to 'explore the psychology of temptation from the *other* point of view', that is from a fiendish viewpoint, in a humorous and profound way.

Screwtape is an elderly devil in 'Hell's civil service' who instructs a younger devil, Wormwood, on the art of temptation. It is this 'demonic' viewpoint, where God is referred to as the 'Enemy' and 'Our Father's House' is not heaven, but hell, which requires the reader to reverse his normal moral viewpoint and see things through the tempter's eyes. Using domestic and commonplace situations to explore the challenges which Christians encounter in their everyday life, Lewis provides an illuminating, and often humorous, account of the snares we often fall victim to.

In describing the strain of having to twist his mind into the diabolical attitude required and of the 'spiritual cramp' which followed the writing of the book, Lewis added that whilst he never wrote anything more easily, nor did he ever write anything with 'less enjoyment'. The book has remained one of Lewis' most popular and entertaining works, and has been given a spirited audio book reading by the English comic actor John Cleese and adapted for the stage.

***Above:** Mansfield College, Oxford* ***Top:** Notice board at Mansfield College welcoming visitors to the chapel*

Above: Fellows' Pews in Magdalen College Chapel, Oxford

'Mr Jack should have been a clergyman'

This was how the caretaker and gardener at the Kilns for thirty-four years, Fred Paxford, described CS Lewis in the pulpit. He recalled Lewis' sermons to a 'packed' Headington Quarry church. His 'full clear voice' could easily be heard and his skilful use of humour when preaching was appreciated by the congregation. Lewis spoke of his Christianity in a number of engagements to various audiences following his conversion.

During the Second World War, the Chaplain-in-Chief of the Royal Air Force, Maurice Edwards and his assistant, Charles

Gilmore, set up a lectureship so that CS Lewis could address members on aspects of the Christian faith. Lewis gave his first talk at the RAF base in Abingdon in May 1941. He revealed in a letter that he thought that they 'were a complete failure,' though he took comfort in the Biblical story of Balaam, 'remembering that God used an *ass* to convert the prophet.'

It was during one of these talks to the men of the heavy bomber squadrons in an RAF chapel in the Norfolk fens that Lewis revealed something of the hostility he experienced at Oxford because of his Christianity. Using the text: 'If any man will come after me, let him deny himself, and take up his cross, and follow me,' Lewis gave a passionate and emotional account of the indignities which Christ endured on our behalf. He then spoke of what it had cost him, as an Oxford don, to be a Christian. He told of the 'intense hostility and animosity'; the unexpected 'ostracism and abuse'; and how he knew what it meant to endure scornful ridicule and vicious intellectual contempt. Even those friends and colleagues who were uncritical regarding his purely intellectual interest in Christianity as a 'subject' for discussion and debate, were indignant that he should actually practise it. The idea that a professor of English Literature could also be famous and successful as an amateur theologian was anathema to many in Oxford.

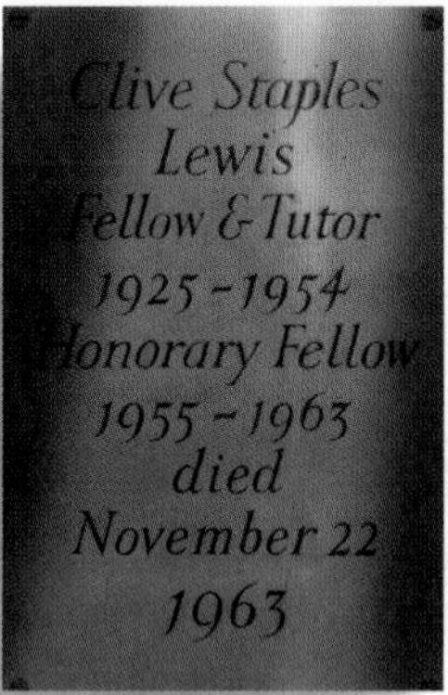

On Whit Sunday, 28 May 1944, Lewis preached a sermon on *glossolalia* (or the gift of speaking in tongues) to a varied audience in Mansfield College chapel, not far from Magdalen. It was an appropriate theme as Whit Sunday, the seventh Sunday after Easter, celebrates the descent of the Holy Spirit upon the first Christians at Pentecost as described in Acts 2. During the sermon, as Lewis spoke of our desire to achieve something approaching St Paul's vision of the spiritual life and how we are ever conscious that we continually fall short, he was so overcome with emotion that he had to leave the pulpit. The principal of Mansfield College went to Lewis' aid and the organist and choir filled the unexpected break with a hymn. By the time the hymn had finished, Lewis had regained his composure and entered the pulpit to resume his sermon.

Not that all Lewis' speaking

Above: *Commemorative plaque in Magdalen College Chapel where CS Lewis would have sat*

Above: In August 1934 Lewis, Mrs Moore, and her daughter, Maureen, took a motoring tour through parts of Ireland, stopping to visit Arthur Greeves, and allowing Mrs Moore the opportunity to meet members of the Lewis family at Martha and Rev. Ranald Muir's home in Newcastle, County Down . First row, left to right: Beth Lewis, Ranald Muir, Joan Lewis, Alex Muir. Back row: Maureen Moore, Ida Lewis, Rev. Ranald Muir, Mrs MT Lewis, Mrs JK Moore, Martha Muir, Sarah Jane Lewis, WH Lewis and CS Lewis

engagements were as emotionally charged as this: he was once asked to address girls of the Royal School, Bath, at a service organised by the future Canon Blair, then chaplain to the RAF camp near Longleat, Wiltshire, in 1945. Canon Blair tells of Lewis holding a 'one-man brains trust', and during his talk he was heckled by the 'school marms' who were in charge of the girls. The question, 'Mr Lewis, can you tell us what hell is like?', brought the instant reply, 'Very like what I am going through now'—at which point a girl fainted! After the inevitable commotion had died down and they returned to resume their questions, Lewis was 'halfway up the Mile Drive of Longleat.'

A happy home

During the course of the war, the Kilns became a temporary home for different groups of three or four evacuated girls, usually from London, who were billeted there. One of the many children evacuated from London during the Blitz was a young girl Jill ('June') Flewett, who arrived at the Kilns during the summer of 1943 and ended up staying nearly two years. In 1950, June married Clement Freud, author, Member of Parliament and grandson of Sigmund Freud, the founder of psychoanalysis. She gives a fascinating insight into life at the Kilns during wartime, and on the relationship between Jack and Mrs Moore, describing how Jack showed Mrs Moore 'the greatest loving care' and how she in turn 'adored him absolutely.' Janie Moore's priority was Jack's happiness and comfort, and life at the Kilns was geared to this end.

Whilst CS Lewis and Janie Moore may have been lovers in the early twenties, by the time Jack had become a committed Christian in the nineteen thirties the nature of the early relationship had changed decidedly. The twenty-six year age gap between the two (together with Mrs Moore's increasing ill-health) meant that when Jack introduced Mrs Moore to his friends as 'mother' or 'my aged mother' he was stating the true nature of their relationship as it had then become. Thereafter she was introduced to friends and visitors simply as 'mother.'

June Flewett's account of Mrs Moore, together with other accounts of those who had actually met her, gives a balanced account that is distinctly lacking in many of the writings on CS Lewis and Mrs Moore. Her observation that 'Mrs Moore and Jack Lewis had happy times together' is a fitting tribute to her time spent in their company. This real-life story of evacuated children staying in a house on the outskirts of Oxford would later provide the inspiration to the

Left: *CS Lewis relished the scholarly atmosphere in the Bodleian Library which he likened to 'the hum of the hive'*

Left: Bronze portrait bust of CS Lewis in the Wade Centre, Wheaton College, Illinois. Photo by permission of the sculptor Lawrence Reid Bechtel

opening chapter of CS Lewis' most famous work *The Lion, the Witch and the Wardrobe*, where the evacuees, Peter, Susan, Edmund and Lucy arrive at the old Professor's house in the heart of the country.

Mere Christian?

Lewis had become a household name due to his wartime radio broadcast talks on Christianity for the BBC. According to *Time* magazine, around 600,000 listened to each of the talks given between August 1941 and April 1944. They had originally been published in three separate volumes and these were eventually gathered together, edited, and published in 1952 as *Mere Christianity*. The title was taken from a phrase of the English Protestant divine and Puritan preacher, Richard Baxter (1615–1691), which was, as Lewis notes, meant to encompass those beliefs which 'have been common to nearly all Christians at all times.'

CS Lewis' story of how he became a Christian is told in *Surprised by Joy: The shape of my early life*. This is not a typical autobiography; one friend even suggested it should have been called 'Suppressed by Jack', due to its lack of candour on certain aspects of his life and conventional autobiographical detail. The book, published in 1955, tells how Lewis passed from atheism to Christianity and how his childhood and adolescence formed him so that the reader may understand the exact nature of his conversion—his 'spiritual crisis'—when it arrives. The whole concept of 'joy' which was so important to Lewis, and dominated his imagination as a young atheist, is now recognised for what it was—a pointer towards God.

TRAVEL INFORMATION

The University Church of St Mary the Virgin, High Street, Oxford

www.university-church.ox.ac.uk
☎ 01865 279111

In the 13th century, the university grew up around St Mary's, which stands in what was then the physical centre of the old walled city of Oxford. The history of the church on this site probably dates from around Anglo-Saxon times. The church hosted part of the trial for 'heresy' of the three Anglican bishops who became known as 'The Oxford Martyrs': Hugh Latimer, Nicholas Ridley and Thomas Cranmer. They were burned at the stake during the reign of the Roman Catholic queen, Mary Tudor. If one climbs the 127 steps to the tower gallery there are marvellous uninterrupted views of the city. CS Lewis preached two sermons in this church in 1939 and 1941.

Mansfield College

www. mansfield.ox.ac.uk
☎ 01865 270999

The youngest and smallest of the University's 39 colleges is situated on Mansfield Road, near New Parks Road and the city centre. CS Lewis preached his famous sermon 'Transposition' here in 1944.

Radcliffe Camera

The first round library to be built in Britain has been described as 'an Orthodox Easter egg'. Named after John Radcliffe, who studied at Oxford and left much of his wealth and all of his medical books to the university. The camera (meaning 'room') was completed in 1749 becoming part of the Bodleian Library. It is now used as reading rooms and is not open to the public.

CS LEWIS WALKIN

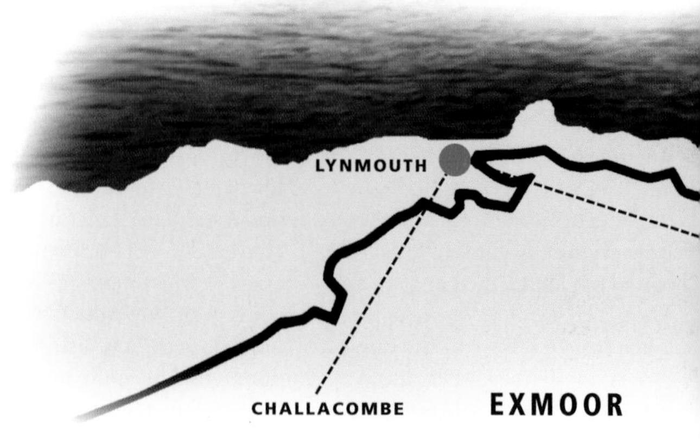

Rycote Chapel, Thame, Oxfordshire

www.english-heritage.org (OS Map 165; ref SP 667046)

☎ 01424 775705

Built in 1449 by Richard Quartermain and used by most of the Tudor and Stewart monarchs on their visits to the nearby Rycote Palace, which sadly no longer exists. The Lewis brothers would visit here with friends. Rycote Chapel is owned by English Heritage and is open to the public on an infrequent basis. The land on which the manor house and Tudor palace stood is now strictly private, but the public right of way (the Oxfordshire Way) runs alongside the chapel.

Woburn Abbey and Park, Woburn, Bedfordshire

www.woburnabbey.co.uk

☎ 01525 290333

Set in the middle of a 3,000-acre deer park, Woburn Abbey has been the home of the Dukes of Bedford for nearly 400 years. Lewis loved to be driven through Woburn Park and enjoyed, in season, the magnificent rhododendron drive and the herds of deer which would wander down to the public highway.

Below: *Detail of the walking tour of 1930, from Dunster to Challacombe in Exmoor*

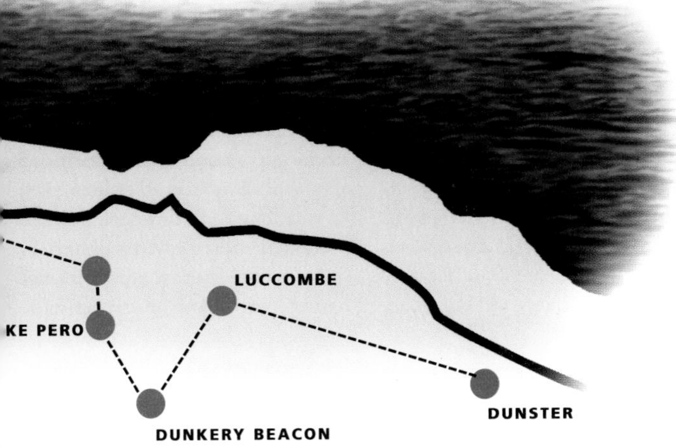

7 Into Narnia

CS Lewis' dreams of lions led to the creation of Aslan, the lion redeemer, of his most famous story *The Lion, the Witch and the Wardrobe*. Just as the Son of God became a man when he came to earth, Lewis imagined that when he went to Narnia, he became a lion

The story of *The Lion, the Witch and the Wardrobe* takes place in England during the Second World War and tells how the four Pevensie children: Peter, Susan, Edmund and Lucy, are sent from London to the remote country house of old Professor Kirke to escape the German air-raids. Just as the child evacuees at the Kilns found their way into the story, Professor Kirke is a thinly-veiled (though much less intimidating!) portrait of Lewis' old tutor, WT Kirkpatrick. Whilst playing a game of hide-and-seek in Professor Kirke's house, Lucy hides in an old wardrobe only to find, as she fumbles about in the darkness, that she has stumbled on an entrance into the magical world of Narnia.

The writing of these stories allowed Lewis to overcome a problem that had plagued him since early childhood in Belfast, 'of feeling obliged' to feel a certain way about God or about the suffering of Christ. This awareness of being told how you ought to feel, actually produced the opposite effect in Lewis, who complained that feigned 'reverence' and an obligation to feel 'can freeze feelings'. By

Above: *'Magical Worlds'. The 1998 Royal Mail stamp of The Lion, the Witch and the Wardrobe*

Facing page: *Detail from the beautiful stained glass window in the University Church of St Mary the Virgin, Oxford where John Wycliffe, John Wesley and CS Lewis preached*

C.S. 'JACK' LEWIS - ULSTERMAN

transferring these things into an imaginary world and divesting them of what Lewis called their 'stained-glass and Sunday school associations', one could steal past those 'watchful dragons' which inhibit our reception of the Christian faith. Lewis' seven Narnian books and three science fiction novels began with 'seeing pictures'. For him, the story of *The Lion, the Witch and the Wardrobe* began with an image of a faun carrying an umbrella and parcels in a snowy wood—which had haunted his imagination since he was sixteen—not by asking himself how he could say something about Christianity to children: 'that element pushed itself in of its own accord'!

Lewis explained in a letter to a little girl how the Narnian story is really all about Christ and that the story grew out of a series of 'supposings': 'Supposing there really was a world like Narnia and supposing it had (like our world) gone wrong and supposing Christ wanted to go into that world and save it (as He did ours). What might have happened?' The whole series of the Narnia books are Lewis' imaginative answer to these 'supposings'.

In a 1961 letter to Anne Jenkins, Lewis summarised the Chronicles of Narnia in relation to the story of Christ like this: *The Magician's Nephew* tells of the Creation and how evil entered Narnia; *The Lion, the Witch and the Wardrobe* deals with the Crucifixion and the Resurrection; *Prince Caspian* tells of the Restoration of the true religion after a corruption; *The Horse and His Boy* relates the calling and conversion of a heathen; *The Voyage of the Dawn Treader* tells of spiritual life (especially in the case of Reepicheep, the valiant mouse); *The Silver Chair* deals with the continued war against the powers of darkness, and *The Last Battle* tells of the coming of the Anti-Christ (The Ape), the end of the world and the last judgement.

The parallels between the Christian story and the history of

***Pictured:** around the sculpture, (shown opposite) set into the block-paving, an engraved border reads: CS 'JACK' LEWIS, ULSTERMAN, TEACHER, CHRISTIAN, WRITER, SCHOLAR. BORN 1898, REBORN 1931*

BORN 1898, REBORN 1931

Above: *CS Lewis' centenary sculpture by the Northern Irish artist Ross Wilson, which stands outside the Holywood Arches Library, East Belfast, not far from Little Lea*

Narnia are skilfully interwoven to create a story that communicates on many levels. These stories are not straightforward allegories, but *supposings*: supposing that there was a magical world like Narnia that needed rescuing and there was only one who could? As the Son of God became a man when he came to earth, supposing that when he went to Narnia he became a lion? Thus, the character of Aslan is not intended to represent Jesus Christ—he is supposed to *be* Christ. These ideas and many of the central truths of Christianity are explored and worked out over the course of the seven books that comprise 'The Chronicles of Narnia.'

Above: *The Searcher uses the literary figure of Digory Kirke from 'The Magician's Nephew' and is modelled on CS Lewis as he was in 1919*

'Once again the axe has fallen'

Mrs Moore (pictured) had become increasingly unwell during the late 1940s and was often in great agony with severe varicose veins and other ailments. The anxiety caused by her illness meant that Lewis' domestic life at the Kilns was often in turmoil—'My aged mother, worn out by long infirmity, is my daily care.' This situation worsened and Mrs Moore, who by now was falling out of bed and needed constant attention, was finally admitted to Restholme, a nursing home on the Woodstock Road in Oxford, in April 1950. Mrs Moore was now aged seventy-nine, and the doctor who was attending her thought that this arrangement would probably be permanent. Jack continued to visit her every day until her death from influenza on 12 January 1951. Her death marked the end of a relationship which had begun in 1917, blossomed against the backdrop of the horror and fear of the Great War and ended with her death over thirty years later.

***Below:** The Narnia Window at Holy Trinity Church, Headington Quarry*

Above: The County Down landscape was central to the inspiration for the landscape for Narnia: walking in the hills around Rostrevor in County Down, Lewis confided to his brother Warnie that this area, which overlooks Carlingford Lough, was his idea of Narnia

The move to Cambridge

In November 1954, CS Lewis accepted the Chair of Medieval and Renaissance English at Magdalene College, Cambridge. In essence this was a result of his outspoken belief in the truth of Christianity. There were of course other factors which contributed to his dissatisfaction with Oxford: changes in the English syllabus, an ever demanding workload, together with his having been passed over for a Professorship on three occasions. Lewis has been described as 'one of the most hated men in Oxford' by senior Oxonians in key positions, on account of his growing popular reputation outside the academic confines of the University.

Dame Helen Gardiner comments that the prejudice among the Oxford authorities against granting Lewis a professorship was due, in some measure, to his commitment to what he himself called 'hot-gospelling', and the fear that this might interfere with the 'administration' responsibilities of the post.

Tolkien noted that in Oxford you are forgiven for writing two kinds of books: your own subject or detective fiction (because even dons get ill and need something to read), but you are not forgiven for writing popular works of theology. He added that Lewis knew this when he accepted the BBC war time invitation for a series of talks on the Christian faith, but he felt compelled by his conscience to do so, even if his popularity as a defender of Christianity worked against his academic career. Lewis' good-natured banter with an acquaintance whose son had got a scholarship to Magdalen in Oxford: 'What has the poor boy done, that you should send him alone and unarmed into that nest of crooks and atheists?' reveals something of his attitude towards his old college.

Lewis' acceptance of the created chair of 'Professorship of Medieval and Renaissance English' at Magdalene College, Cambridge, was, some argue, an embarrassment to the Oxford authorities, who, realising their mistake, tried to make amends by creating a new chair and offering that to Lewis—but it was too late. Lewis had made up his mind. Rather than being thought of as the 'fogey' and 'old woman' of 'leftist, atheist and cynical Magdalen' he might, he muses, become the *enfant terrible* of 'pious, gentle and conservative'

Left: *Lewis took up residence in Magdalene College, Cambridge, in January 1955*

Below: *Punting on the River Cam as seen from Magdalene College*

***Above:** Lewis' rooms (the five arched windows from the left) were above the Parlour and Old Library at Magdalene College, Cambridge*

Magdalene.

The historian GM Trevelyan presided over Lewis' inaugural lecture and revealed that this was the only university appointment in the whole of his experience for which the electing committee had voted unanimously. In his first lecture, *De Descriptione Temporum* (Latin for 'a description of the times'), Lewis argued that the pre-Christian and the Christian have more in common than with the modern non-worshipping post-Christian. Closing the lecture he claimed that 'Old Western Culture' was practically dead and that he was among the last of the 'Old Western Men'—'a dinosaur.'

Surprised by Joy!

Joy Davidman was the daughter of middle-class, non-religious Jewish immigrants. Born on 18 April 1915, she and her brother Howard were brought up in the Bronx area of New York City. She describes how she and her brother 'sucked in atheism with their canned milk', due to the dominating influence of her atheistic father, who put great pressure on his children to succeed academically. She wanted to be a writer from the age of twelve, and after finishing her formal education Joy went on to publish her first literary work in 1938, a volume of poetry entitled *Letter to a Comrade*. This was followed by two novels, *Anya* (1940) and *Weeping* Bay (1950). She declared herself an atheist at eight after reading HG Wells' *Outline of History*, and she professed communism in 1938.

Whilst attending a Communist Party function in 1942, Joy Davidman met William 'Bill' Gresham, a divorced, one time

Above: *Interior of Magdalene College Chapel, Cambridge*
Below: *The plaque in Magdalene College Chapel commemorating CS Lewis*

folk singer in Greenwich Village nightclubs, freelance writer, and fellow communist. He was a veteran of the Spanish Civil War, and returned from the experience disillusioned, depressed and alcoholic. Gresham was a deeply troubled man who attempted to mask this by cultivating a charming personality. He obviously made an impression on Joy for they were married in August that same year.

Both soon became disillusioned with communism and Joy thereafter devoted herself to raising her two sons, David, born in 1944 and Douglas a year later. The trauma of her husband's mental breakdown in 1946 led her to confess that for the first time in her life she felt 'helpless'. The experience led her to a spiritual encounter with God when her worldly defences of 'arrogance and cocksureness and self-love behind which I hid from God, went down momentarily. And God came in.' Joy soon found herself on her knees praying—'the world's most astonished atheist.'

By 1948 both Joy and Bill had embraced Christianity and were attending a local Presbyterian church. The story of their separate conversions can be found in *These Found the Way: Thirteen Converts to Protestant Christianity* (1951).

Bill Gresham remained deeply troubled and soon abandoned whatever grasp of Christianity he had; first for Scientology and later, Buddhism. Their marriage was not to be a success, primarily because of Bill's alcoholism and persistent infidelity and, following various attempts at reconciliation, Bill and Joy were finally divorced in August 1954.

It was during this difficult period in her marriage that Joy Gresham began a correspondence with CS Lewis which was to have such a profound effect on both their lives. In this correspondence she was encouraged by her friend Chad Walsh, an Episcopalian minister and writer of the first book ever published on Lewis, entitled *CS Lewis: Apostle to the Skeptics* (1949). Joy first wrote to Lewis in January 1950, attracting the praise of both Jack and Warnie Lewis for her 'amusing and well-written letters' and before long they had become pen friends.

In August 1952, Joy sailed to England, with the express intention of meeting CS Lewis, and she stayed with another pen friend, Phyllis Williams, in London before visiting Oxford, where they invited CS Lewis to lunch with them in the Eastgate Hotel, just across the street from

Below: *The Pepys Building which houses the Bibliotheca Pepysiana, or the Samuel Pepys' Library, which was received by Magdalene College, Cambridge in 1724. It is reported that Lewis only visited the library once whilst at Cambridge and then only on the insistence of two eminent Oxford friends who were visiting him*

Magdalen College. Several days later Lewis returned the compliment and invited them to dine with him and his brother at Magdalen College. Warnie had to cancel this engagement and Jack's friend George Sayer stood in for him. It was not until later that year that Warnie and Joy met for the first time. Warnie, though initially hesitant, was impressed with her and a rapid friendship developed.

Joy remained in England for the next five months working on her new book *Smoke on the Mountain*–an interpretation of the Ten Commandments–which she discussed with Lewis and who would later write a foreword to it. She also accepted an invitation to spend two weeks with the Lewis brothers at their home, the Kilns, during the Christmas holidays of 1952. Joy showed Jack the letter she had just received from her husband Bill, saying that he and her cousin Renée were in love and asking for a divorce. She initially hesitated, but later agreed and on her return to the United States in January 1953, commenced proceedings which would lead to a final divorce in August 1954.

Joy returned to England with her sons, aged nine and seven, in April 1953 and lived in a two-room ground floor flat in London. They stayed with the Lewises at the Kilns for four days in December that year, which Jack enjoyed, though he found the energetic stamina of the American boys and the entertaining 'very, very exhausting.' Jack and Joy appear not to have seen too much of each other from this point, apart from the Greshams staying at the Kilns during the summer and Christmas holidays of 1954. It was not until Joy and her sons moved to a house in Headington, Oxford, about a mile from the Kilns, in August 1955 that they began to see each other on a regular basis. Lewis had been working on his autobiography since 1948 and by the time it was published in 1955 his original title *Surprised by Joy* had taken on a whole new meaning—giving rise to the popular observation: 'Did you hear what's happened to CS Lewis? He's been surprised by Joy!'

***Above:** Joy Davidman in 1960*

To marry for a visa

When Joy had her visa refused in April 1956, Lewis offered to marry her in a purely formal civil ceremony that would satisfy legal obligations and allow her to claim British citizenship so that she and her children could stay

Above: *The Pickerel Inn, a favourite of Lewis and his friends is directly opposite the entrance to Magdalene College in Cambridge*

permanently in England. Jack insisted to a friend that it would not be a 'real marriage', he liked and admired her, but was not in love with her, and that the whole thing should be kept a secret lest people misunderstood. It was on this basis that the marriage between CS Lewis and Joy Gresham took place in the Register Office in St. Giles, Oxford on 23 April 1956.

Within two months of this marriage for a visa, Joy had suddenly fallen ill and by October that year she was diagnosed as having cancer in various locations, with her left femur almost eaten through. The illness was to bring a profound change to both their lives.

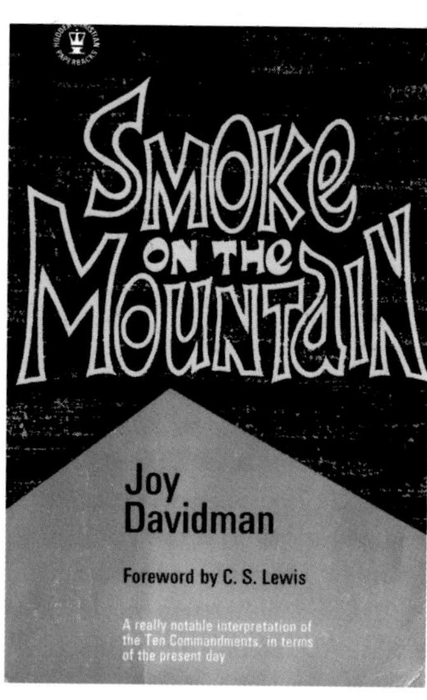

Above: *Joy Davidman's book, 'Smoke on the Mountain'—an interpretation of the Ten Commandments*

***Left:** Mill Lane Lecture Hall, Cambridge, where CS Lewis gave his inaugural professorial address 'De Descriptione Temporum' on his fifty-sixth birthday in 1954*

***Right:** 10 Old High Street, Headington, Oxford The house where Joy Davidman and her two young sons lived in Headington, Oxford in 1955*

TRAVEL INFORMATION

Magdalene College, Magdalene Street, Cambridge

www.magd.cam.ac.uk
☎ 01223 332100
The College of St Mary Magdalene is located in the centre of Cambridge beside the bridge on the River Cam, from which the city takes its name. Magdalene was founded by Benedictine monks and dates from 1428. There is a plaque in Magdalene College Chapel commemorating Lewis' time there. Lewis preached a sermon here, 'A Slip of the Tongue', on 29 January 1956. Through the Second Court of Magdalene College is the Pepys Building which houses the pride of Magdalene—the Samuel Pepys Library, his private collection of 3000 books. Samuel Pepys (1633–1703) is possibly best known for his famous diary of London life from 1660 to 1669 which includes an account of the Great Fire of London in 1666.

***Above:** Pepys Library*

Christian Heritage Cambridge, The Round Church, Cambridge

Opposite St John's College
www.christianheritageuk.org.uk
☎ 01223 311602
Specialising in guided tours, walks, and promoting a knowledge of our Christian heritage. The church was built in 1130 and is one of only four medieval round churches in England. The second most visited location in Cambridge. Located at the junction of St John's Street and Sidney Street.

King's College Chapel, King's Parade Street, Cambridge

www.kings.cam.ac.uk
Guided tours are available through the Cambridge Tourist Office. ☎ 01223 457574
The Chapel is the grandest and most beautiful attraction in Cambridge. King's College was founded by Henry VI in 1441 and the Chapel was completed in 1547. When Lewis first saw King's College Chapel he found it 'beautiful beyond hope or belief.'

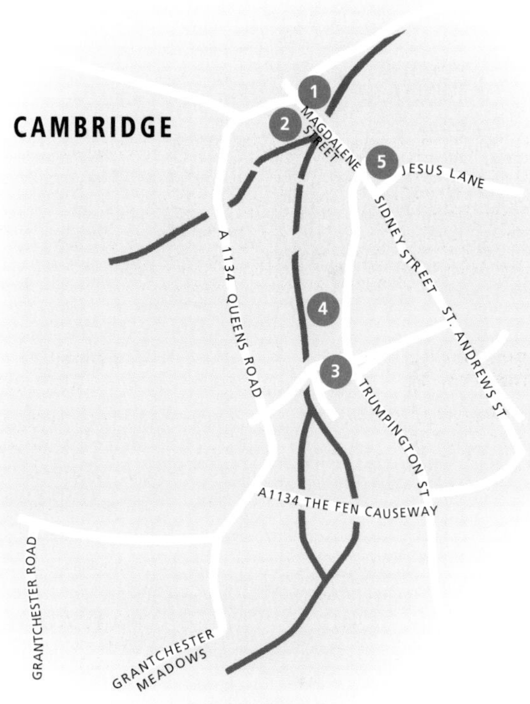

KEY TO PLACES

1 MAGDALENE COLLEGE
2 THE PICKEREL INN
3 MILL LANE LECTURE HALL
4 KING'S COLLEGE AND CHAPEL
5 ROUND CHURCH

King's College, Cambridge

8 Through the Shadowlands

The tragic story of CS Lewis' marriage to a terminally ill woman, her temporary recovery and her eventual death from the same disease which had claimed the lives of his own parents, challenged the Christian faith of Lewis in the most painful way

In November 1956, Joy had three separate operations to remove the cancer. It was obvious to Jack that she could not possibly care for herself, so it was agreed that she should move into the Kilns and that their recent, hitherto secret, marriage should be made public so as to avoid scandal. On Christmas Eve, 1956, the London newspaper *The Times* announced that 'A marriage has taken place between CS Lewis of Magdalene College, Cambridge, and Mrs Joy Gresham, now a patient in the Churchill Hospital, Oxford. It is requested that no letters be sent.'

Although Jack and Joy dearly wanted an ecclesiastical ceremony, the Bishop of Oxford, Harry Carpenter, though sympathetic, refused as the official Church of England position on remarriage forbade it. Furthermore, the Anglican Church as the Established Church recognised their Registry Office marriage as being valid and therefore could not allow them to be married twice.

Lewis did not see the force of these arguments and appeared hurt and upset. With Joy's health continuing to deteriorate, he asked a former pupil and friend, the Rev Peter Bide, who had something of a reputation as a healer, to lay hands on Joy. Bide arrived at the Kilns on the night of 20 March 1957 and shortly after his arrival, Jack explained his dilemma and of Joy's wish to receive the marriage sacrament before she died. Lewis asked Bide to marry them. His friend asked for time alone to consider the matter. Bide had no jurisdiction in the Diocese of Oxford and he knew that the marriage would be a grave breach of church law. However, he considered Jack a 'special case' and felt an intellectual debt and the natural obligation towards a friend. He finally asked himself what Jesus would have done in such a situation, and that, he thought,

Facing page: *Ballymastocker Bay and Portsalon in County Donegal. When CS Lewis brought his new bride to Ireland in 1958 their delight in the beauty of the country provided a welcome temporary relief from the worry of Joy's illness*

'somehow finished the argument.' Bide married the couple the following morning in Joy's room in the Wingfield-Morris Hospital, with the Ward Sister and Warnie Lewis as witnesses. Following the marriage, Bide laid hands on Joy and prayed.

Above: *Front door of the Kilns*

A miraculous healing?

The following month, April 1957, Joy was sent home to die at the Kilns. What happened next was what Lewis described as the nearest thing to a miracle he had ever experienced—Joy began to get better. The cancer was arrested, then gradually began to disappear. Within a few months Joy, who previously was in such agony that she had to be carefully moved in bed by three people, could walk with the aid of a stick. Within a year the man who took the last x-rays of Joy was

Below: *The Kilns as it is today. The house was bought by the CS Lewis Foundation of Redlands, California, in 1984 and the restoration of the house was begun in 1993*

Above: *Warren Lewis' typewriter. Warren acted as his brother's secretary for many years and undertook the mammoth task of editing the eleven volumes of the family history, 'Memoirs of the Lewis Family: 1850–1930*

exclaiming, 'These bones are solid as a rock. It's miraculous.' Lewis thought it was a case of what his friend and fellow Inkling, Charles Williams called, the 'Way of Exchange or Substitution'—where individuals can accept into one's own body the pain of someone else. Jack now discovered that he also had a bone disease, osteoporosis, and that he 'was losing calcium about as fast as Joy was gaining it, and a bargain for which I'm very thankful.' He found that as the pain left Joy's body, he could feel it entering his: 'It was crippling. But it relieved hers.'

Joy continued to make remarkable progress in her recovery and she started to turn the Kilns into a home. The fact that Jack and Warnie's friends referred to the Kilns as 'The Midden' (or 'dunghill') gives some idea of the state of the place prior to Joy's arrival. It was she who organised its decoration for the first time in thirty years, despite fears that removing the overflowing bookcases might collapse the walls! She also took an active interest in Jack's work, and her suggestions and advice helped

Jack overcome 'writers block' with a novel he was working on.

This was one of the happiest periods in Jack's life and he remarked to a friend: 'I never expected to have, in my sixties, the happiness that passed me by in my twenties.' The couple enjoyed a 'belated honeymoon' in Ireland–'a perfect fortnight'–during July 1958, visiting Counties Louth, Down, and Donegal, returning 'drunk with blue mountains, yellow beaches, dark fuchsia, breaking waves, braying donkeys, peat-smell, and the heather just beginning to bloom.'

A Grief Observed

With Joy's health continuing to hold, the couple repeated their previous year's schedule and visited Ireland again in July 1959. However, within a few months, the news that they always expected, but were never really prepared for, finally arrived. Following a routine check at the Churchill Hospital, X-rays showed that Joy's cancer had returned in various parts of her body. Joy was intent on fulfilling her ambition of visiting Greece, despite her increasing pain, and she argued that if Jack would risk it, they should proceed with their

Left: The Old Inn, Crawfords-burn, County Down. The couple stayed a week here during their honeymoon in 1958 where Joy was introduced to Jack's relatives

Above: View from Portsalon harbour, near Rathmullan, County Donegal. CS Lewis holidayed in the Portsalon area and his poem 'Star Bath' was possibly inspired by his time there

holiday. When they decided to go, both knew that Joy was dying and each knew that the other knew this. It was with this poignant knowledge that in April 1960 they travelled to Greece with their friends (and future co-biographer) Roger Lancelyn Green and his wife June. They enjoyed eleven days visiting Athens, Rhodes, Crete, and other sights, before returning, via Pisa, to London. Lewis summed it up: 'Greece was wonderful.'

The following month, Joy underwent surgery on the 20 May 1960 to remove a cancerous growth in her breast and the following month she returned to the Kilns. Her health continued to deteriorate and, apart from a brief reprieve, she spent the last weeks of her life in at times painful but relative calm. Joy woke screaming in agony on the morning of 13 July 1960 and was rushed to the Radcliffe Infirmary. 'You have made me happy' and 'I am at peace with God' were two of her last comments to Jack as she slipped in and out of consciousness. Joy died peacefully in Jack's company that night around ten o'clock. On Monday 18 July, 'a sunny, blustering day, with big white clouds,' Joy was cremated at Oxford Crematorium. Jack's version of his poem 'Epitaph', written especially for Joy, is engraved on a marble plaque near the place where her ashes were scattered.

Joy's death left Jack emotionally stunned. Following the advice he once gave to a friend that 'ink is the great cure for all human ills', during the first few months following his wife's death Lewis recorded his distress in the starkest terms in a journal. The book was written under the pseudonym NW Clerk: NW is an abbreviation of Nat Whilk, Anglo-Saxon for 'I know not whom' and Clerk meaning scholar or writer. It was later published in September 1961 as *A Grief Observed*. The book draws on some of the range of raw emotions Lewis felt in the aftermath of Joy's death: anger, fear, self-pity, and despair, all surface as the author attempts to cope with his loss. He comes to realize that you can't see, or deal with, a situation properly 'when your eyes are blurred with tears.' Working his way step by step through his sorrow, he finally arrives at a deeper understanding of God, the nature of grief and his own limitations. Lewis comforted his grieving teenage step-sons as best he could in the aftermath of their mother's death. The Kilns remained their home during this difficult period: David attended Magdalen College School as a day boy, whilst the younger Douglas continued boarding at Lapley Grange school in Montgomeryshire, Wales.

Remember
HELEN JOY
DAVIDMAN
D. July 1960
Loved wife of
C.S. LEWIS

Here the whole world (stars, water, air,
And field, and forest, as they were
Reflected in a single mind)
Like cast off clothes was left behind
In ashes, yet with hope that she,
Re-born from holy poverty,
In lenten lands, hereafter may
Resume them on her Easter Day

Three months after Joy's death, Jack was back in his normal working routine at Cambridge and spending weekends at the Kilns. His health had suffered, and during Joy's final weeks he had been diagnosed with an enlarged prostate gland. This was to cause Jack much discomfort and he was scheduled for surgery, but his general state of health would not allow the operation. He was put on a strict regimen which required that he change his diet and give up tobacco. He reluctantly changed his eating habits, but would not give up smoking, thinking it better to 'die cheerfully with the aid of a little tobacco, than to live disagreeably without.'

Lewis' habits of moderate beer drinking and smoking have raised eyebrows among some Christians. The son of the founder of Bob Jones University in Greenville, South Carolina, Dr Bob Jones Jnr (like Lewis, a 'hot-gospeller' of some repute) met CS Lewis in Oxford in the 1940s. Jones has written of Lewis that 'in conversation, he gave a very good personal testimony of his own faith in Christ' and when asked what he thought of Lewis, replied—'That man smokes a

Above: *The epitaph for Joy Davidman written by CS Lewis*

Left: *Jack and Joy spent the second week of their honeymoon in Rathmullan, on the shores of Lough Swilly in North Donegal. View from Rathmullan Priory built c. 1508*

pipe. That man drinks liquor, but I *do* believe he is a Christian!'

The term is over

Apart from a brief return to Cambridge, Jack spent the next few years recuperating at home reading and revising his unfinished manuscripts. During a blood transfusion at the Acland Nursing Home on the 15 July 1963, Jack suffered a heart attack and went into a coma. He woke from this the following day, surprising both visitors and doctors, and his health seemed gradually to improve over the next few weeks. Reluctantly, he had to cancel his plans to bring his stepson, Douglas, to Ireland for a holiday.

Realising that he would be unable to return to work, Jack resigned his position at Cambridge on 14 August 1963. His beloved brother Warnie had returned to the Kilns in October and the brothers were aware that Jack was nearing the end of his life. They turned to each other for comfort then as they did when they were children in the 'little end room,' and shut out the knowledge that, in Warnie's words, 'a new term fraught with unknown possibilities awaited us both.' The 'new term' came around five thirty on Friday 22 November 1963, when Warnie, hearing a crash in Jack's room, rushed in to find him lying unconscious.at the foot of the bed. Clive Staples Lewis died some three or four minutes later. Jill Flewett Freud, who was one of the child evacuees at the Kilns in 1943, had arranged to visit the Lewis brothers for a few days and rang within thirty minutes of Jack's death only to be told the awful news by a stunned Warnie. His death was overshadowed by the news that, on the same day in Dallas, Texas, President John F Kennedy was assassinated.

The Christian legacy of CS Lewis

The fact that many of Lewis' religious writings are imaginative and purely speculative should be borne in mind when considering his religious beliefs. For this reason alone he cannot be easily pigeon-holed. For Lewis, no such problem of classification arose. 'The guiding thread in all my books,' he wrote, was that 'the imaginative man in me was older, more continuously operative, and...more basic than either the religious writer or the critic.' Lewis repeatedly declared that when he spoke on theological matters it was as an amateur and not as an 'expert' or professional

Mere Christianity

An extract from one of Lewis's most powerful conclusions in *Mere Christianity.*

'I am trying here to prevent anyone saying the really foolish thing that people often say about Him: "I'm ready to accept Jesus as a great moral teacher, but I don't accept His claim to be God." That is the one thing we must not say. A man who was merely a man and said the sort of things Jesus said would not be a great moral teacher. He would either be a lunatic—on a level with the man who says he is a poached egg—or else he would be the Devil of Hell. You must make your choice. Either this man was, and is, the Son of God: or else a madman or something worse. You can shut Him up for a fool, you can spit at Him and kill Him as a demon; or you can fall at His feet and call Him Lord and God. But let us not come with any patronising nonsense about His being a great human teacher. He has not left that open to us. He did not intend to.'

Above: *The hand-carved wardrobe by the grandfather of Lewis which provided the inspiration for the Narnia stories*

Above: CS Lewis' career at Magdalene College, Cambridge was cut short by illness in 1963

theologian. He saw his task as a *translator*—one who turns the essential doctrines of Christianity into everyday language that everyone can understand. When Lewis came to edit the BBC radio broadcast talks for publication (as *Mere Christianity*) he found he had very little rewriting to do because his writing style reflected his confidence in the spoken word—or as he succinctly put it, 'If you cannot put your faith in the vernacular, then either you don't know it or you don't believe it.'

Lewis claimed that most of his books were 'evangelistic' and that it would have been inept, on his part, to 'preach forgiveness and a Saviour to those who did not know they were in need of either.' He argued that the Christian conversion of a country, or even a single soul, requires 'an alteration of the will' and that this alteration could only come about by 'supernatural intervention.'

Lewis drew the analogy of the role of the Christian apologist as being comparable to that of John the Baptist, whilst the Preacher, the Evangelist, 'the man on fire, the man who infects', represents the Lord Himself'. He remained throughout his adult life a member of the Church of England and, despite some ingenious attempts to portray him as a closet Roman Catholic, he assured a correspondent: 'No I'm afraid I'm not even an Anglo-Catholic, I'm a Protestant.' Realising that his

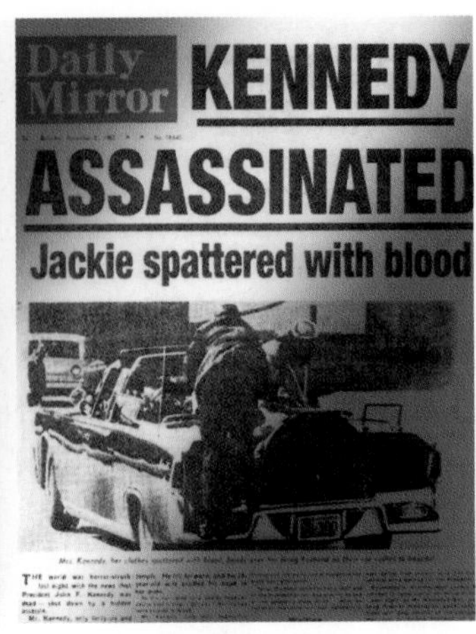

Daily Mirror

KENNEDY ASSASSINATED

Jackie spattered with blood

Above: *The death of CS Lewis (above), on 22 November 1963, was overshadowed by the assassination of President Kennedy*

usefulness as a Christian 'depended on my having kept out of all dog-fights between professing schools of "Christian" thought. I'd sooner preserve that abstinence to the end.'

'God in the Dock'

In his essay 'God in the Dock', Lewis drew upon the difficulties he experienced as a speaker to RAF and student audiences in 'trying to present the Christian Faith to modern unbelievers.' He was aware that his work as an evangelist suffered to an extent from 'the incurable intellectualism of my approach'. Whilst the simple emotional appeal to 'come to Jesus' was often successful in bringing many to Christ, he admitted that he 'lacked the gift' for making it. This perceived 'weakness', if we may call it that, was in fact one of Lewis' greatest strengths. He recognized that his usefulness as a communicator lay in his ability to disentangle the nuances of language, which in the minds of his audience may mean a number of different things, and to arrive at an agreed and precise linguistic meaning. Only then, when a common understanding was established, could the rationale and truth of the gospel be laid plainly before all.

It was in this ability to turn aspects of belief and doctrine into everyday speech that Lewis excelled. To convince his audience of modern unbelievers, many with 'an almost total absence from the mind of any sense of *sin*,' that they were in fact 'guilty' before God, Lewis had first to 'convince our hearers of the welcome diagnosis, before we can expect them to welcome the news of the remedy.' That the remedy lay in the saving power of the Lord Jesus Christ is embedded in all of Lewis' work following his Christian conversion.

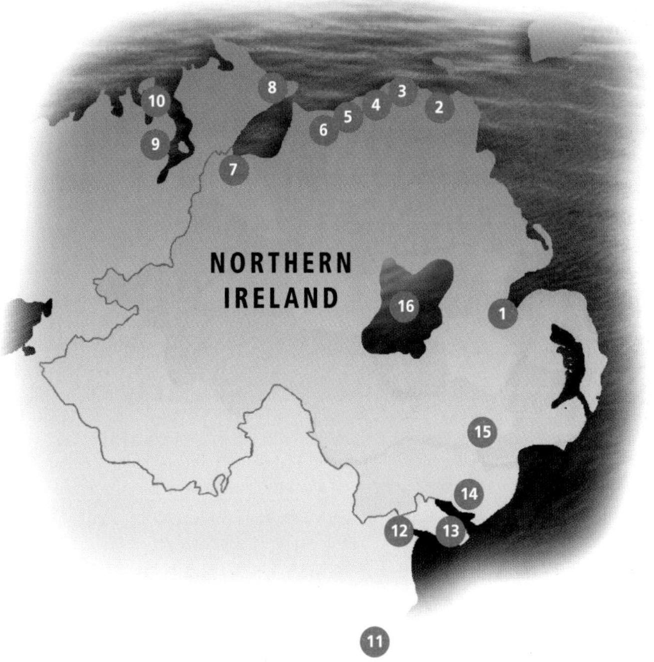

NORTHERN IRELAND

TRAVEL INFORMATION

Oxford Crematorium and Garden of Remembrance

Bayswater Road, Oxford.
☎ 01865 351010
The funeral service of CS Lewis' wife, Helen Joy Davidman, took place here on 18 July 1960. Joy's memorial plaque is located towards the far end of the garden walkway at the rear of the chapel. Bayswater Road is the smaller, fifth road running off the Green Road roundabout to the north-east.

Above: *The gravestone of CS Lewis and his brother at Holy Trinity Church, Headington* *(see page 83)*

KEY TO PLACES

1 BELFAST
2 BALLYCASTLE
3 GIANT'S CAUSEWAY
4 PORTBALLINTRAE
5 DUNLUCE CASTLE
6 CASTLEROCK/DOWNHILL
7 LONDONDERRY
8 MOVILLE
9 RATHMULLAN
10 PORTSALON
11 DROGHEDA
12 DUNDALK
13 CARLINGFORD
14 ROSTREVOR
15 MOURNE MOUNTAINS
16 LOUGH NEAGH

A Summary of CS Lewis' life

29 November 1898	Clive Staples Lewis born in Belfast.
21 April 1905	Lewis family moves from Dundela to 'Little Lea'.
23 August 1908	Death of his mother, Flora Lewis.
18 September 1908	Lewis enrolled at Wynyard School, Watford.
September to November 1910	At Campbell College, Belfast.
January 1911	At Cherbourg House, Malvern.
April 1914	Lewis meets Arthur Greeves and his private tutor WT Kirkpatrick.
6 December	Lewis confirmed by his grandfather, Rev Thomas Hamilton, at St Mark's, Dundela.
August 1916	Arrives in Belfast and holidays with Arthur Greeves in Portsalon, County Donegal.
1917	At University College, Oxford.
8 June	Lewis joins Army and is gazetted into Somerset Light Infantry.
17 November	Crosses to France and arrives in the trenches on 29 November (his nineteenth birthday).
15 April 1918	Wounded in Battle of Arras. Paddy Moore, who had been missing in action since 24 March, reported dead in the same month.
11 November 1918	Armistice signed.
13 January 1919	Returns to Oxford after a period of convalescence in English hospitals.
20 March 1919	First collection of poems *Spirits in Bondage* published.
14 and 21 March 1921	Meets with WB Yeats.
1 August 1922	Takes up residence with Mrs Moore and her daughter at Headington, Oxford.
20 May 1925	Elected Fellow of Magdalen College.
18 September 1926	*Dymer* published.
25 September 1929	Death of his father, Albert Lewis.
23–24 April 1930	Lewis and his brother at Little Lea for the last time.
Christmas Day 1931	Lewis takes the necessary 'leap of faith' and proclaims his Christian conversion by taking his first Communion since childhood in his parish church at Headington Quarry, Oxford.

15–29 August 1932	Writes his first prose work, *The Pilgrim's Regress*, whilst on holiday at Arthur Greeves' home in Belfast.
25 May 1933	*The Pilgrim's Regress* published.
8 August 1933	The Lewis brothers arrive in Belfast to view the stained glass window in St Mark's that they commissioned in memory of their parents.
31 July–31 August 1934	Lewis, Mrs Moore, and her daughter, Maureen, take a motoring tour through parts of Ireland, stopping to visit Arthur Greeves, and allowing Mrs Moore the opportunity to meet members of the Lewis family.
3 September 1939	War declared.
6–27 August 1941	Lewis gives four broadcast talks on 'Right and Wrong' over BBC.
June 1947	In Ireland for a short holiday with Arthur Greeves. This was the first time the two had met since the summer of 1938.
16 October 1950	*The Lion, the Witch and the Wardrobe* published.
12 January 1951	Death of Mrs Moore.
24 September 1952	Lewis meets Joy Gresham.
7 January 1955	Takes up residence in Magdalene College, Cambridge.
19 September 1955	Lewis' autobiography *Surprised by Joy* published.
23 April 1956	Lewis and Joy Gresham married.
19 October 1956	Joy admitted to hospital suffering from cancer.
21 March 1957	Lewis and Joy are married in a hospital bedside ceremony.
June 1958	After a period of recovery, Joy's cancer is diagnosed as being arrested.
October 1959	Joy's cancer returns.
13 July 1960	Death of Joy Davidman Lewis.
August 1960	Lewis writes *A Grief Observed.*
24 June 1961	Falls ill with enlarged prostate gland.
15 July 1963	Admitted to hospital with a heart attack.
22 November1963	Death of CS Lewis, a week short of his 65th birthday.

Select list of works by CS Lewis

Poetry

1919 *Spirits in Bondage: A Cycle of Lyrics*
1926 *Dymer*
1964 *Poems*, (edited by Walter Hooper)
1969 *Narrative Poems*, (edited by Walter Hooper)

Books for Children

1950 *The Lion, the Witch and the Wardrobe*
1951 *Prince Caspian*
1952 *The Voyage of the 'Dawn Treader'*
1953 *The Silver Chair*
1954 *The Horse and His Boy*
1955 *The Magician's Nephew*
1956 *The Last Battle*

Academic

1936 *The Allegory of Love: A Study in Medieval Tradition*
1942 *A Preface to Paradise Lost*
1948 *Arthurian Torso*
1954 *English Literature in the 16th Century Excluding Drama*
1960 *Studies in Words*
1961 *An Experiment in Criticism*
1964 *The Discarded Image: An Introduction to Medieval and Renaissance Literature*

Autobiography

1955 *Surprised by Joy: The Shape of My Early Life*
1961 *A Grief Observed*

Christian Writings

1933 *The Pilgrim's Regress*
1940 *The Problem of Pain*
1942 *The Screwtape Letters*
1946 *The Great Divorce*
1947 *Miracles*
1949 *The Weight of Glory*
1952 *Mere Christianity*
1958 *Reflections on the Psalms*
1960 *The Four Loves*
1964 *Letters to Malcolm: Chiefly on Prayer*

Science fiction

1938 *Out of the Silent Planet*
1943 *Perelandra*
1945 *That Hideous Strength*
1977 *The Dark Tower & Other Stories* (edited by Walter Hooper)

Novels

1956 *Till We Have Faces*

Letters and diaries

1966 *Letters of CS Lewis*, (edited by Warren H Lewis)
1967 *Letters to an American Lady*, (edited by Clyde Kilby)
1979 *They Stand Together: Letters to Arthur Greeves*, (edited by Walter Hooper)
1985 *Letters to Children*, (eds. Lyle W Dorsett and Marjorie L Mead)
1989 *Letters, CS Lewis/Don Giovanni Calabria: A Study in Friendship*, (edited by Martin Moynihan)
1991 *All My Road Before Me: The Diary of C.S. Lewis 1922–1927*, (edited by Walter Hooper)
Hooper, Walter (ed.) *C. S. Lewis: A Companion and Guide* (HarperCollins, 1996)
Hooper, Walter (ed.) *Collected Letters, vol. 1 Family Letters 1905–1931* (HarperCollins, 2000)
Hooper, Walter (ed.) *Collected Letters, vol. 2 Books, Broadcast and War 1931–1949* (HarperCollins, 2004)

For further reading

Bresland, Ronald W. *The Backward Glance: C. S. Lewis and Ireland* (Institute of Irish Studies, 1999)
Carpenter, Humphrey *The Inklings* (Harper Collins, 1997)

Kilby, Clyde S. and Mead, Marjorie Lamp

(eds.) *Brothers and Friends: The Diaries of Major Warren Hamilton Lewis* (Harper & Row, 1982)
Schultz, Jeffrey D. and West Jnr, John G. (eds.) *The CS Lewis Readers' Encyclopedia* (Zondervan, 1998)

ABOUT THE AUTHOR

Dr Ronald W Bresland is one of the leading authorities on CS Lewis' Irish life and background. He was formerly a Cultural Traditions Fellow at the Institute of Irish Studies, The Queen's University of Belfast (1997–1998). His book *The Backward Glance: CS Lewis and Ireland* (1999) explored the many connections between CS Lewis and Ireland. He has lectured and contributed to documentaries on CS Lewis in the UK and US and has written the Northern Ireland Tourist Board brochure 'Northern Ireland: The CS Lewis Story' (2005). He is currently working on an illustrated book *CS Lewis: An Irish Companion.* Ronald, who lives in County Tyrone, is the father of five children and is married to Catherine. See below for website.

ACKNOWLEDGEMENTS

The Lion, the Witch and the Wardrobe 1998 © Royal Mail Group plc. Reproduced by kind permission of Royal Mail Group plc. All Rights Reserved.

Arts Council of Northern Ireland

The Belfast Natural History and Philosophical Society

Photographs by kind permission of the President and Fellows of Magdalen College Oxford; University College, Oxford; Magdalene College, Cambridge; British Red Cross Museum and archives;and the CS Lewis Foundation, Redlands, CA.

Raymond Compton

Sir Richard Dunbar

Ron Humphreys

Beth Tate

TBF Thompson

Illustrations on p. 54 and p. 80 by kind permission of Ross Wilson

Tony Wilson

The Public Record Office of Northern Ireland for photographs D/4185/A/1,3,4,6,[9,6],10,14,17 on pp. 11,13,27,7,32,67,44,4.

SELECT LIST OF WEBSITES

Northern Ireland Tourist Board Official website: **www.discovernorthernireland.com** has DVD and links to the CS Lewis story.

St. Mark's Church, Dundela, Belfast: **http://dundela.down.anglican.org** has a valuable guide to CS Lewis' associations with the church.

Those wishing to hear **CS Lewis' voice** can purchase the audio books *The Four Loves* and *CS Lewis Speaks his Mind* from **www.alliance4media.org**

Famous people of Headington: **http://www.headington.org.uk**

The author's web site: **www.cslewisinireland.com** will continue to explore CS Lewis's links with Ireland.

KEY TO PLACES IN MAINLAND UK

(SEE PAGE 123 FOR NORTHERN IRELAND)

1 OXFORD 2 WATFORD 3 WHIPSNADE 4 WOBURN ABBEY 5 CAMBRIDGE
6 MALVERN 7 CAERGWRLE/HOPE/HAWARDEN